Cathy Forde was born in Glasgow and taught English in secondary schools and colleges as well as working as a lexicographer before turning to writing full time. Her novels include *Bad Wedding*, *Dead Men Don't Talk* (both Barrington Stoke, 2009); *Fat Boy Swim*, *Skarrs*, *Firestarter*, *The Drowning Pond*, *Tug of War*, *Sugarcoated* (all Egmont Books, 2003–2008); *L-L-L-Loser* (Barrington Stoke, 2006); *I See You Baby* (with Kevin Brooks, Barrington Stoke, 2005); *Exit Oz* (Barrington Stoke, 2004); *Think Me Back* (House of Lochar, 2003); and *The Finding* (House of Lochar, 2002). She has won both the Grampian Book Award and the Scottish Arts Council Award, and is the 2009–10 Virtual Writer in Residence for Teens and Young People with the Scottish Booktrust. *Empty* is her first stage play. Her second play, *The Sunday Lesson*, will be produced in Oran Mor, Glasgow, as part of their Spring 2010 'A Play, A Pie, A Pint' season.

Published by Methuen Drama 2010

1 3 5 7 9 10 8 6 4 2

Methuen Drama
A & C Black Publishers Limited
36 Soho Square
London W1D 3QY
www.methuendrama.com

Copyright © Cathy Forde 2010

Cathy Forde has asserted her rights under the Copyright,
Designs and Patents Act 1988 to be identified
as the author of this work

ISBN: 978 1 408 13057 5

A CIP catalogue record for this book is available from the British Library

Typeset by Country Setting, Kingsdown, Kent
Printed and bound in Great Britain by
CPI Cox & Wyman Ltd, Reading, Berkshire

Introduction

What do you do when Vicky Featherstone, Director of the National Theatre of Scotland, invites you to a meeting and offers you a commission on the spot?

- Pinch yourself?

- Say 'Yes, please!'

- Quake with terror inside?

- All of the above?

In May 2008, this was the extraordinary situation in which I found myself.

'Just go away and write a play,' I was instructed. About anything. The merest hint of a brief came with Vicky's suggestion that I try to create something that might entice young people to the theatre of their own volition.

No pressure then . . .

Actually, gargantuan pressure. Not only had I never written any drama in my life before, but it was years since I had even sat in the audience at someone else's play. Work, family and the hassle-factor of being seated in time for a 7.30 p.m. curtain up all conspired to make the thrill of attending live theatre a broken habit and a distant memory.

But what a difference a year and a half makes. Mentored, inspired and enthused by Frances Poet, Literary Manager of the National Theatre of Scotland, I have become reconnected with an experience I have missed out on for far too long. Not only did I return to attending live theatre whenever possible, but Frances recommended I repair the chasms in my knowledge of contemporary drama by reading Brian Friel, Conor McPherson, Martin McDonagh, Philip Ridley, Douglas Maxwell, David Greig, Anthony Neilson . . . I dutifully devoured every playtext she recommended and every few weeks we met and discussed my 'homework'. I felt as if I had enrolled for a crash course in Contemporary Drama with an excellent tutor to support me, only a tutor who never set critical essays to hand in for assessment.

So all this was enormous fun. Throughout the summer months of 2009 I didn't read a single novel, only plays. I didn't miss novels one little bit either, growing to relish the *distillation* of a story or situation into a far more visceral, stripped-back form.

I knew that when – eventually – I knuckled down to the first draft of my own first play, this distillation, this cutting to the quick of what was happening, would be my aim. There could be no luxury of slow unfolding, no protracted scene-setting, nothing extraneous. Only: *pow: this is now.*

That was my aim. That was how I wanted this play to turn out. Distilled. Sharp. Visceral. Lean. Obviously, that was not what I achieved, certainly not in the early drafts of *Empty*. It was my first play, after all, and I was coming to it as a novelist where you have the luxury of time to create a world in all its minor details and subplots and meanderings. Some of the tools in my prose writer's kitbag just didn't quite fit the job in hand, and learning to adapt these tools has been my biggest challenge as a fledgling playwright.

Interestingly, however – and fortunately – the singular most crucial element to the creation of *Empty* developed exactly the same way as all my other stories so far. That crucial, essential element is always the germ of an idea. Unless it pings into my head, and seeds and roots, there is no story. And if there is no story, there is nothing.

Luckily, the almost throwaway brief suggested to me when I was commissioned gave birth to my germ in this instance: devise a story that might lure young people to the theatre along with other 'regular' theatregoers. Whatever I wrote had to be inclusive, therefore had to be something with which everyone could identify. (And crucially, crucially, crucially what I wrote must on no account be written specifically 'for' a teenage audience. I never, ever do that; it is patronising.) And that's when I had my 'ping': I would write about an unparented teenage party, or as it's called in my neck of the woods, an

'Empty'. Teenagers host Empties, attend Empties, and if they don't, they hear about them. Parents – despite what their kids think – hear about Empties too, and dread them, mainly because – despite what their kids think – they were all guests at Empties themselves in their own youth. They know exactly what goes on. Oh yes. And what can happen to their offspring and their property . . .

So there was my story; I would write a play about an Empty.

It started as a much denser – and longer – play, the novelist in me unable to resist creating a complex back story. Early drafts introduced Col and his friends, not as sixteen-year-olds, but ten years on from the night of the party at the centre of this play. They were all mid-twenties, evolving into adults and bearing, in varying degrees, repercussions from the night of Col's summer Empty. Col had two extra friends – decent, responsible guys, Chas and Fingers – whose maturity was the foil to Stevie and Fiona's self-centred recklessness. With these somewhat passive characters cut, Bella's broad shoulders carry the heart and kindness in the play.

Col's parents also existed as living characters in the first two or three drafts of the play, but as I was nursed through discussions about what this play, this *story*, was really about, its essence gradually crystallised. Bit by bit, inessential padding fell away to reveal what – for me, and I hope for anyone reading the playtext or watching – *Empty* is all about.

And what is *Empty* about? Well, I *think* it's about one young person who is in a state of *becoming*. In one night of his life, a chain of events that he has not the power, the will nor the strength of character to influence, tilt the course of his future irrevocably. Change the man he might have become.

And it's about a mental teenage party.

Cathy Forde

Empty

Empty was first performed by the National Theatre of Scotland at the Tron Theatre, Glasgow, on 12 March 2010, before touring to the Brunton Theatre, Musselburgh, the Eden Court Theatre, Inverness, and the Lemon Tree, Aberdeen. The cast was as follows:

Col	Ben Presley
Lily	Charlene Boyd
Stevie	Ross Allan
Bella	Sally Reid
Fiona	Shabana Bakhsh

Director Vicky Featherstone
Designer Georgia McGuinness
Lighting Designer Natasha Chivers
Sound Designer Mark Melville

Characters

Col, *an everylad*
Bella, *a big broth of a lassie; has a misguided sense of fashion for
her build*
Stevie, *an arse with charisma*
Lily, *pert, groomed, sexy, and does she ever know it*
Fiona, *snide, tarty, worldly wise*

All characters are sixteen to seventeenish.

An empty set.

Enter **Col**, **Bella**, **Lily** *and* **Stevie** *in school uniform.*

Facing the audience, the group sings 'Beautiful Tomorrow' (Mahalia Jackson). The performance affords each character a small solo.

Col's *performance is straightforward.*

Bella *is much better than she realises.*

Lily *is self-aware – an actor playing a girl in a choir.*

Stevie *sings passable falsetto and emotes as if he is in a private fantasy where he is a serious contender on a prime-time TV talent show.*

When the song is done, the lights go down.

Lights up again. **Col** *is centre stage, the others standing about separately in the background.*

As **Col** *addresses the audience, he seems to bear more age.*

Col   OK. This is out there, right, but sorta just need to let you . . .

I dunno . . .

See the shit *this* lot all get me into . . .

Lily   *Excuse* me!

Stevie   Us?

Col   Mean, what I'm saying is, 's not like we plan . . .

Well, *I* don't.

Wouldn't.

No way. This was landed on me.

Just got caught up in the –

Stevie   You reckon?

Col   And I don't want you all leaving here, right?

Looking at me.

Judging.

Thinking: 'What a shower o' . . . '

Bella   Destructive.

Stevie   Wasted.

Lily   Thoughtless.

Col   Selfish, depraved, sordid, disrespectful, untrustworthy, spineless . . .

Shit, cuz it's not like that.

Not meant to be. We're just young.

Just a few randomy singing pals from –

All   'Compulsory Extra-Curricular Elective'.

Col   – who end up . . .

Beat.

Hey, and right now we've all just finished our exams. Got that . . .

Y'know, that summer feeling?

Know what I'm talking about? Enda term.

All improvise elation.

Col   When life feels like it can't get any better.

Nothing but time ahead to look forward to.

And this is our *now*.

None of us know we're on the –

Lily   Cusp.

Col   Man, in't she always got the perfect – ?

Stevie   Everything.

Lily   *Bon mot.*

Col   Look at her. She's . . . she's . . . *aw* . . .

Stevie   Hose yourself down, horny boy.

Lily   – *cusp.* We're on the cusp.

Stevie, **Lily** and **Bella** *muster to exit.*

Col (*addressing audience*)   Christ on a bike. I'm sixteen. Six foot, six inches –

Stevie   Ya wish.

Col   All my own spots.

Bella   School's out.

Lily   Today!

All (*singing à la Alexandra Burke*)   Halleluia!

Bella (*exiting*)   So happy holidays, guys! Better all be into the caff to see me. Save me going off my chump. Punt you free poky hats and extra raspberry.

Exit **Bella**.

Stevie (*making to exit in opposite direction*)   So I will, Bella. Drop in special just to cop a swatch at the sweat dripping offa your big shiny red face.

Bella (*off*)   Shut it, Stevie.

Lily (*looking at* **Col**)   And I would if I could but I can't, Bella. But, don't worry, I'll think about you in España. Only two days to go!

Stevie   Awright for some. Don't get skin cancer.

Or crabs offa some skanky wee Spic cocktail waiter.

Exit **Stevie**.

Col   What's he like, eh? Fuckwit.

Lily   Nah, harmless. Cheeky chappy.

Col   Think?

Lily   Mhhh.

Col   Offski to Spain then?

Lily   Day after tomorrow. Me and Fi –

Col   Going with *Fiona*.

Lily (*in a breathless gush*)   I know. Wild. Don't know what my mum's thinking letting me. Can you imagine? Staying in this massive villa. Pool and terrace and Fi's crazy mum totally loved up with her latest toyboy. Be able to do anything we like, me and Fi. And we will. Totally deserve it too. Cuz straight down to Cornwall after. Three weeks with the heinous family –

Col   So won't see you all summer.

Lily   How will you survive? Will you pine?

Col   I'll miss you.

Lily   And I'll miss you too, Colly-Wolly.

Col   No. I *will* miss you. Loads.

Lily   Me too.

Col   Will you?

Lily   Course.

Col   Honest?

Lily   Mhhh.

Col   Honest?

So . . .

Well . . .

Actually . . .

Thinkin' . . .

Kinda know what . . . ?

Like howz about . . . ?

What if mibbe . . . ?

Well, you and me . . .

We could . . .

Lily   What? Spit it out. Say what you're trying to say like Stevie would if he was in your shoes right now.

Col   You fancy coming over to mine, Lily?

Lily   What, like *now*?

Col   'F you want.

Lily   But I'm still in my *uniform*, Col! God's sake. Ginging.

Col   Looks fine to me.

Lily   Not the point. Sweltered in it, amn't I?

Col   Later then.

Whatever you want.

Any time.

Change. Come back.

Lily   For?

Col   Nothing. Mean, hang out just.

Sunbathe –

Lily   *Sun*bathe? So what you're trying to say is you wanna see me in my brand new itsy-bitsy pinky-winky teensy-weensy flimsy-wimsy bikini?

Col   No. Yes. No. Course I do.

If you want. That'd be mint.

Only if you want.

Do anything you want.

Beat.

Stay over if you like.

Lily   Stay over?

Col   If you like.

Lily   Hang on. What about Mummy Knox?

Doubt she'd approve of *that*.

Col   'S awright. Out.

Lily   *Out?*

Col   Her and Dad.

Lily   Where out?

Col   Somewhere for her birthday. Just hit five-oh.

Lily   Awww.

Beat.

Where?

Col   Largs or something. For the day, like.

Lily   So why're you inviting me to stay overnight at yours if she's coming back?

Pause.

Col, just tell Lily: have Mummy and Daddy Bear gone away for a filthy dirty sexy weekend somewhere?

Col   Largs.

Said.

Lily   So where they really?

Beat.

Col   London. Fancy hotel. Musical and shit.

Lily   Oooh. *Mamma Mia? Les Mis?*

Col   How the fuck d'I know. Fucked off. Away. Out my hair.

Lily   And the mice can play, that's all that matters. *Eeeek, eeek, eeek*. All night long.

Col   Yeah.

Yeah.

So you'll come round later? And stay. Long as you want.

Mean, they won't actually be back till Monday.

Lily   Three nights to yourself!

Col   Well, not if you're here.

Lily   Mean, basically you've an end-of-term empty –

*As **Lily** says the word empty, **Bella** and **Stevie** walk around the stage and peel away the black masking that conceals the outline of a room drawn on the floor. While **Lily** and **Col** speak, **Stevie** and **Bella** hang a window at the back of the set and lay cards/labels on the floor outside the outline indicating the other unseen areas of **Col**'s house, e.g. kitchen, garden, bedroom).*

Col   Eh, no –

Lily   – and you've kept all mum about it, naughty, naughty boy.

Col   Hey. No. Serious, Lily. I'm not letting on.

Promised.

Cuz shit, Mum'd pure epi it if I –

Lily   Col, Mum'd never know. Got days to clear up. Be fine after.

Col   Won't be fine after! Never is –

Lily   Will if you ask the responsible people.

Like me and Fi.

And Stevie –

Col   Responsible? Stevie? He's a bammy balloon.

Anyway, empties are never responsible.

Lily   We'll call it 'Lily's Away-All-Summer' party. Boo hoo.

Col   Lily, I'd love to have a party for you –

Lily   Knew it. You're the best.

Col   – but I can't.

Lily   And I'd lu-u-u-u-v you to have a party for me.

Think about it . . .

Col   Look, I can't.

Lily   How grateful I'd be.

How I'd show you how grateful I'd be.

Col   Still can't . . .

Lily   Ooooh, think how much I'd lu-u-u-u-v you for it.

She is excited.

A bientôt.

Col   Just you, Lily.

Listening?

Exit **Lily**.

While **Col** *delivers the following monologue,* **Bella**, **Stevie** *and* **Lily** *begin to furnish the space* **Col** *is standing in until a sitting room is created.*

Stevie *and* **Bella** *carry on a sideboard. It is placed along the back wall.*

Bella *and* **Lily** *bring on sofas.*

Stevie *wheels on a big flat-screen telly and carries in a record player.*

Bella *brings in a stack of classic vinyl records.*

Bella, **Stevie** *and* **Lily** *bring on and arrange elaborate bouquets, gift-wrapped bottles, fiftieth-birthday cards to Mum and family photographs on the sideboard.*

Col   Empty.

Fuck. No chance.

Life wouldn't be worth living after. She'd land me the full court martial and a firing squad.

(*Mimics his dad.*) 'And no more than you deserve either. You've been well warned, boyo. No shenanigans. I know the likes of you young people: whenever three or more of ye are gathered unsupervised it's melted tellies and melted heads all round. Canny help yourselves. No self-control at your age. I know. Was young once myself, remember. So make sure you don't have your mother walking into an aftermath.'

(*Mimics his mum cruelly.*) 'Oh, Jesus, Mary and Joseph, Col, I couldn't be coping with it. Bad enough hearing the stories you hear without them coming to life in your own front room. I told you about Jean from work?'

That'd be Permed Jean.

(*As his mum.*) 'Yes, Permed Jean. Well, her daughter not only had them taking the strip of co-caine before they were allowed over the door into the shindig she threw behind her mother and father's back, but she had them snorting it off their own naked bodies instead of the mirrors you're supposed to use when you take the strips of co-caine. Y'know?'

Actually I don't, Mum.

Mean, who needs the hassle of clearing up pals of pals of pals' shit on your own doorstep?

And.

There.

Will.

Be.

Shit.

Always is. Fuck that for a game of soldiers.

Mean, tonight this house is mine, all mine. And Lily might well be too by the end of it.

Fuckin' mint!

To raucous music, **Col** *takes frenzied ownership of the sitting room, during which he helps himself to drinks from the top of the sideboard and changes for his big night with* **Lily**.

To the side of the stage **Bella**, **Stevie** *and* **Lily** *can also be seen changing into their party gear.*

When **Col**'s *dance winds down, he slumps on the sofa, then homes in on the sideboard, expertly by-passing the lock by removing a drawer to produce a bottle of vodka*

Col   'Snifter, sir?'

'Don't mind if I do, Jeeves.'

'Make it a double.'

'Righty ho, sir!'

'Bottoms up.'

Rubbish! Not even a fuzzy headrush in that pathetic dribble.

Chucks bottle away. Finds gunky advocaat.

Forget your ancient eggy shit, but, Mum – blah! No wonder you've been complaining your guts are fucked up.

Aha, more like it.

Produces couple of gift-wrapped bottles. Opens one of whisky. Toasts Mum's photo.

Though a young shaver like meself shouldn't be drinking alone.

Man, really hope she's coming. Soon.

Col *sweet-talks an imaginary* **Lily**.

Col   'Well hello there, sexy lady. Lookin' good enough to gobble . . . '

No, no . . . that's pushing my luck. 'Lookin' good enough to eat.'

'Listen. Honest, you are the finest . . . '

Col *steers imaginary* **Lily** *to sofa.*

Col   'Park your assets, sweet-cheeks . . . '

No. Wank.

'Just sit yourself down on the settee there, hen.'

OK. OK. Calm.

'Oops. Something on your shoulder, Lily.'

Nah. Twat.

Dandruff, she'll think.

Say hair.

'Oooh. Greenfly, is that? Let me just flick it . . . '

'Looking forward to Spain then?'

'Me?'

'Nah hameldae me. Abroad always gives me skitters anyway.'

Fuck. Don't say that, pie. She won't come near you.

Doorbell.

Col   Ya beauty!

More persistent doorbell.

Shit! Someone's keen.

He checks breath, hair, underarms. Gulps some whisky. Exits.

Door being thumped now, letterbox flapping.

Lily (*off*)   Hi-ya!

Col (*off, in silly voice*)   Well a-come on in, baby.

Enter **Lily**.

Col   Here you are!

Lily   Here I am. Ta-da!

Col   Wasn't totally sure you'd come, to be honest.

Lily   Colly! What d'you take me for? Wouldn't miss this for the world.

Col   Really?

Lily   Start of the hollys, Colly.

Oooh, I'm so excited.

Col   Brilliant! I'm excited too.

So d'you want to sit down?

Or maybe get a drink?

Take it upstairs.

Doorbell.

Col   Mhh?

More persistent doorbell.

Col   Who'd that be?

Lily   Oooh, let's go see.

Exit **Lily** *followed by* **Col**.

Shrill excited girl voices off.

Enter **Fiona** *with alcopop carryout.*

Fiona   Aye, smashing to see you an' all, Knoxy.

Enter **Col** *with* **Lily**.

Col *makes 'what's she doing here?' gestures at* **Fiona**.

Fiona (*aside to* **Lily**)   Thought you said Stevie Hepburn'd
definitely be round by the time we –

Lily (*diverting* **Col** *by flashing her bikini*)   Ta-ra, by the way, Col!
As promised: peek-a-boo!

Look, Fiona's got hers on too for you.

Fiona (*flat, flashing bikini top*)   Peek-a-boo.

Col   What's that 'bout Stevie?

(*Sotto voce to* **Lily**.) 'S just meant to be –

Lily   What? How mean is that, Col?

First night of the hols? Expect me to dingy Fifi?

Fiona   This better not be *it*. Two on one, and he's the one.

Coulda been doin' an extra Fake Bake –

Lily   Anyway, Col. Look at you, all pure dressed in your little
tight summer shirty.

Dun't he look sweet, Fi?

Fiona   'F you say so. Dun't exactly look in party mood, but. Whassup, choirboy?

Lily   Oooh, he's in a party mood now Lily's here –

Col   Why'd I be in a party mood?

Lily   – aren't you Colly-Wolly, my bestie best friend in the whole wide world?

And looking so hot. (*Arms out for hug.*)

Col (*returning hug distractedly*)   That's cuz I *am* hot.

Sodding boiling.

Could go into the garden. Be in the shade.

(*Whispers.*) Get rid. Just us. Only two loungers. She might just leave –

Lily   D'you want to come and sit in Col's garden, Fifi?

There's two loungers.

Fiona   Joking? With the midgies eating the face I've just put on and that slimy coffin-dodger next door pure gowping evils over the fence.

Col   Aw, you never said anything rude, did you?

Fiona   As if?

Flashed my tits, that's all.

Lily   She did too!

Fiona   So that's Grandad happy-happy, and so'll I be an' all. Once Knoxy dishes me some nice bubbly like a proper mine host.

Fiona *indicates all the gift-wrapped bottles.*

Col   Not your host.

Fiona (*shaking up champagne*)   C'mon. How's about it, party boy?

Col   I can't open them!

Fiona   Do it for you then, Mr Muscle.

She starts opening champagne. **Col** *tries to stop her, but the cork pops and champagne spills over both their hands and the carpet.*

Fiona/Lily   Ooooh!

Col   Shit, now look what you've –

Fiona   Aye, watch the shoes!

Lily   Ooops.

Fiona   I name this party –

The girls toast.

Lily   Col's Surprise Champagne Bash!

Fiona   Knoxy's Pop-Your-Cork Party.

If you're lucky.

Lily   Col's 'There's-No-Party' Party.

Fiona   Knoxy's 'Aye there is now, laughing boy, like it or lump it' party.

Col   Not funny. Gone spilt that all over the –

Fiona   A splash! And look.

Rubs in invisible.

Nearly.

Lily   Mummy won't know, Col.

Fiona   And that's the cork out now.

Lily   No going back.

Fiona *slugs and passes to* **Lily**, *who drinks.*

Fiona (*sings tunelessly and dances round* **Col**)   So 'Let's just make this a night to remember.'

Lily   Cheers! Ooooh, Col. Tonight's *sooo* gunna set us up for España.

Your 'Guerilla Empty', that's what we should call it.

Col   What?

Lily   Oooo, do I *love* you!

Hey, so still don't believe Col's *the cohones* for *fiesta*?

Fiona   Whit?

Lily   *Cohones*.

One of the Spanish words you were looking up 'stead of sticking your eyelashes on.

Fiona   Zat the blowjob?

Lily   Fion-*ah*!

Fiona   Oh. Aye. Baws? No.

Still looks more like he's hosting a funeral party, but.

Col   Oi, listen. Please gunna drink up and just fuckin' –

Doorbell and knocking.

Fuck's that now?

He exits with bottle.

Fiona   About time! Losing the will to live and I'm only in the door.

Stevie (*off*)   Col's the king of the castle. Open up, you sleekit rascal. Part-ay!

Oi, wot you staring at, Grandad? Never seen sex on legs at close range before?

Fiona   Whooo! Here comes the cavalry.

Stevie (*off*)   Hey, Knoxy, m' brother from another mother. Look at you, tanking into the good stuff already. That's what I'm talking about! So what's the deal with ol' fanny baws next door?

Enter **Stevie** *with carryout, followed by* **Col**.

Col   Oi, where d'you think you're . . . ?

Why you . . . ?

Stevie   Put him straight, so I did: 'Shouldn't you be dead, Gandalf?'

Col   Said what?

Stevie (*shouting in* **Col**'s *face*)   'Shouldn't you be dead, Gandalf?'

Hey, hos! Heeere's Stevie!

Lily/Fiona   Hi-ya.

Stevie   Hey, know what, Col? I'm a genius –

Fiona   If you say so.

Stevie   See, even before Lily texted me: 'Git your glad rags on and your smokin' hot little ass over – '

Col   Lily texted you?

Lily   'Smoking hot little ass.' As if.

Hey, lovely flowers, eh?

Stevie   'Water them' on Mummy's list?

Col   List?

Stevie   Col's 'stuff to do while Mummy and Daddy have went and left him on his wee tod' list.

(*To* **Lily**.) Where is it they've went again for the day: Largs?

Col (*to* **Lily**)   You told him?

Stevie   On Lyin' Air.

Col (*to* **Lily**)   You told him Mum and Dad were away?

Lily   Well, they are! When I texted him he asked.

Stevie   Listen, still trying to tell you, but you're getting all aerated. See, even before Lily the Pink texted my official invite –

Col   What invite?

Stevie   – I *sensed* you were being michty cagey 'bout your end-of-term plans tonight.

'Chillin' it,' you tells me.

Fuckin' lies, methinks to meself.

'Aha, Mish Moneypenny, shere ish shomeshing afoot.'

Fiona   Did you wheech suss it, Stevie?

Stevie   Aye, I did too.

Pure perceptive at picking up vibes like that. Could do that Most Haunted dobber's job, no sweat.

Sher is an empty house about to be, so I thought.

Sher ish de location for the partification –

Col   Stevie, fuck's sake. Juiced or wasted or . . .

And – fuck – what's with the stupit jock-collar up?

Stevie   Oi, top-notch threads these, man.

Fiona   Never mind that, where's the top-notch talent you promised Lily you'd –

Stevie   On their way.

Col   What talent?

Aw hey. She better not mean your bampot footie crew –

Stevie   Oopsies!

Col   Serious! And see 'f you've noised up Mr Berry over by.

Lily   Fifi flashed him.

Stevie   What with? Imaginary tits?

Fiona   'Member that! When you're begging a feel for real.

Col   Knows fine I'm not allowed any –

Stevie   Colly Wolly Doodle, man. Few deep breaths, eh? In. Out. In. Out. Might be wasted, but least I'm not wired. Here –

He holds champagne to **Col**'s *mouth.*

Drink! Anyhow, see if the whole team crash the choirboy's, they'll only be (*cowboy voice*) passin' through –

Col   Can they not just pass by?

Stevie   – sayin' 'Howdy-doody! happy holidays!'

Fiona   Better be passing through soon, 'fore I pass out from lack of stimulation.

Stevie *is worrying the sideboard lock.*

Stevie   Ey, Fort Knox this.

Fiona   Fort *Knox*, hahaha.

Col   Yuck it.

Stevie   How?

Col   Break it.

Fiona   And can't have Mummy knowing you were a naughty choirboy.

Lily   She won't.

Stevie   You're right, she won't. So just postpone the breakdown, man.

Not even know we've been here. Dib dib. Promise –

He has to raise his voice over a rumpus off – doorbell etc.

Col   What was that?

Stevie   – though like, *I'm* staying here for the duration, but see mosta that lot –

Hey, I'd let them in, by the way. 'Fore they get rowdy.

Fiona   Too right!

She exits.

Stevie   Aye, but see that lot: no worries.

They're only fuelling up for crashing Slammo's sister's yooni pal's eighteenth.

Fiona (*off*)   Hello, boys!

Stevie   Know who I mean? Piggy big minger. Wanna see her.

Col (*at door*)   Listen, there's about a dozen folk already I hardly know ramming their way into the kitchen −

Stevie   Actually you don't. Bella school.

Or should that be Bella stable −

Lily   Ste-*vie*. Hey, did I text Bella?

Col   Did you?

Stevie *groans.*

Lily   The more the merrier.

Stevie   Cookin'! We'll've this joint stoked way up to eleven before anyone leaves, man −

Col   Really prefer you didn't −

Stevie   Mean, check it in here so far. Talk about ancient fuckin' civilised! (*Mincing*) Banter. Chat. Drinky poo. How are you?

Lily   And no music.

Stevie   Sort that easy enough.

He flicks through records.

Col   Oi!

Stevie   Pile a shit this shit, by the way.

'Hippies and Saddoes: the Ultimate Collection.'

Col   Gunna not touch.

Stevie   How? Only looking, man.

Col   Just gunna not. I'm not even allowed to touch them.

Stevie   All in order, is they?

Col   Mibbe. Hey, and that's my mum's favourite album.
Gunna watch.

Sound of glass breaking off.

Col, *in doorway, is torn between records and rumpus.*

Col (*at door*)   Oi!

Lily   Ooopsies!

Col   Bugger.

Fiona (*off*)   In't the goalie meant to be a pair of safe hands?
That's two bloody litres of Strongbow splooshed all up my legs
now, clumsy.

Col (*from door*)   Never mind your legs. What about the floor?

Fiona (*off*)   Only kidding. Wipe me dry and I'll forgive you.

Lily   What's she like?

Stevie   Pure stunt bike.

Col (*off*)   Is no one cleaning that up?

Stevie (*flicking through records*)   Why make work for yourself
this early on?

(*To* **Lily**.) Christ, you and Raleigh Chopper in Spain together,
man? What a team. Slapper and tickle.

Lily   Ste-*vie*! Fiona's my *friend*.

Stevie   Anybody's friend, tip enough Smirnoff Ice down her
scragger.

Col (*off*)   Oi. Mate. Gunna just not shake that can and . . .

Aw, that was *crystal*, that glass.

Dunno who told you anything was happening cuz you're all
gunna have to –

Stevie (*addressing sitting room*)   I sez there was a party.

And there is whether you like it or not, so (*whines*) 'gunna stop' gurning.

And you shoulda let us into your secret sooner. 'D've supplied more Niblets.

He necks some whisky.

Enter **Fiona**.

Stevie, **Fiona** *and* **Lily** *at sideboard. Behind* **Col***'s back* **Stevie** *dismantles Mum's bouquets, adorning the girls and obscuring Mum's photo with greenery.*

Stevie   Soor-mugged SuBo's putting me off my party stride. Face on it only a mother could –

Lily   Love?

Stevie/Fiona   Huv.

As others crack up at the pun, enter **Col**.

Col   Shift your jocks, man, gunna? Totally rubbering me.

Aw, hey! They're Mum's.

Stevie   'Ey're Mum's.' Everything in here's like fuckin' Mum's, innit.

Lily   Don't these look oodlies better on me than in Mummy's vase?

Fiona   Check it: we're Queens of the Party.

Stevie   Be dead by the time she gets back anyway.

Col   Not the point! Look, wish you'd just fuck off out.

Lily   Me? You invited me, Col.

Col   Nah, you can stay.

Fiona   Going nowhere if she's staying. Pal!

Stevie   And I'm crew! And Lily said I had to come.

Col   She did?

Lily *Peut-être.*

Col But you didn't say come to that crew through there.

Stevie No, that would be me. On Lily's instruction.

Col Well, they're pure causing mayhem now. Climbed up on the counters 'n –

Stevie Aw, chill the chips, man.

'Ve said, (*sings*) we're 'movin' on up' soon as –

Col – 'cluding big Sandy, face down on the kitchen floor.

Fiona In two litre of my good cider –

Sounds of vomiting, then cheering off.

Col In his own boke?

He protests from door.

Fiona Jeezo, gunna get some sound going? Drown his winging.

Pure doing my napper.

Stevie and **Fiona** *start strewing records from their sleeves.*

Lily (*mocking*) Care-*ful*! They're in order.

Stevie (*flinging records over his shoulder*) Nothin' but shite.

Col (*off*) Aw! Not the *rug.* Sheepskin.

Stevie Yoof of today. Canny hold a bucket.

Exit **Col**. *Immediately re-enters.*

Col Sandy fuckin' Dick.

Lily/Fiona Dick the sick.

Col I'm not going out there again.

Enter **Bella**, *Guinness in hand.*

Bella (*examining soles of shoes suspiciously*) Aw, what is this?

Lily Belle of the ball!

Stevie   Lock up your daughters!

Bella (*to* **Lily**)   So your text wasn't another wind-up.
What the fuck, Col?

Stevie   Du-uh! Prayer meeting, Bella.

Bella (*ignoring* **Stevie**)   Death wish, have you? Your mum's
even more of a Kommandant than mine.

Col   And fuckin' knobend Dick's just puked all over her
fuckin' kitchen.

(*To* **Stevie**.) Oi, told you. They're in alphabetical order –

Fiona   – of shit.

Stevie   Arsewipe. Bollocks. Crap. Doo. Excrement. Faeces . . .

Col (*to* **Bella**)   Anyway, how d'you get in? Didn't hear the
bell.

Bella   Er. Door. Pure gaping. Hall heaving. And someone
better swab that floor 'fore your Mum's carpet gets all tramped
in with – (*fulsome vomit mime*).

Stevie   Not my problemo.

Col   Whose then?

Stevie   You need to calm down. Here. (*Offers pill.*)

Lily   Sweeties!

Col (*slapping pill away*)   You need to put *them* back in order.
Now.

Stevie   Zeig heil, Son of Kommandant!

Sounds of more vomiting off, plus laughter and squealing.

Col (*at window*)   Man, there's dickhead Dick out spattering
the path, now.

Bella (*tidying up records*)   Chase him.

Stevie   Don't exactly think he can run right now, hen.

Bella   Want me to chase him?

Stevie   That *would* get him sprinting right enough: 'It's the Blubbery Bella Blob Monster. Get me outa here?'

Col   Think you can chase them all?

Stevie   Nae danger: flash your muffin top, Lugosi. Clear the decks in one fell swoop.

Fiona   Girl-friend!

Lily   Ste-*vie*!

Bella (*to* **Col**)   Zat what you want?

Everyone who's come to go?

Lily   Colly-Wolly, you can't! Booo.

Stevie   Wouldn't advise it, pal.

Beat, in which everyone looks to **Col**.

Stevie   That's the spirit!

He hands **Col** *a drink.*

Stevie   Hey, you don't even need to quit this room to party hard.

Col   What?

Lily   I know. Look.

Bella   Pure heaving with the good stuff, right enough.

Could all get gonged out our trees.

Col   Bu –

Bella   *Could*, saying.

Lily   Champers isn't your poison, Bella.

Stevie (*his* **Bella** *impression*)   'Pure poof's drink that, man.'

Col (*his* **Bella** *impression*)   'Gie's a pint of Guinness and Bailey's!'

Col/Stevie   'Guinleys!'

Bella   Don't talk like that.

Col/Stevie (*joint* **Bella** *impression*)   'Naw?'

Bella   No.

Lily   Boys! Hey, look at all this lovely jubbly bubbly, though.

Col   Tip of the iceberg that. Sideboard's crammed too.

Gunna take a million years to get tanked, rate my folk tipple.

Stevie (*sings*)   And that's what friends are for.

Hey, relax. Look.

Stevie *and* **Col** *moving from door to window.*

Stevie   Chilled down already out there.

Bella   Not chilled down enough. Sweltering tonight.

Sweat's pure trickling.

D'you get this?

Lily   What?

Bella   Like puddles of wet.

Wee sticky pools.

In the crease behind your knees?

Lily   No!

Fiona   Eh, never.

Bella   See?

Fiona   Must we?

Lily   TMI.

Bella   Just saying it's boiling.

Alphabetical, yeah?

Bella *continues sorting records. but in her bustling way she steps on one that is still in its sleeve and breaks it.*

Col (*at door*)   Aw, beam me up. Here's frizzy Roisin and *her* squealy mates!

Behind **Col**'s *back the others freeze in shock at the accident as* **Bella** *draws the broken record from its sleeve*

Stevie   Foot in the door, and she scores!

Bella (*mouthing*)   Fuuuuck . . .

Fiona (*chants quietly*)   I'm tellin', you're smellin'

Lily, **Fiona** and **Stevie** *slink out,* **Stevie** *whipping the record sleeve from* **Bella** *as he exits.*

Col (*at door*)   *Hate* that bunch – all clomping through the spew in their stupit high . . .

Not kidding, Bella, see Mum – she's gunna major thrombo.

And my dad.

Bella   Where they away to really? Lily said Largs.

Col (*shrug*)   London. *Mamma Mia* and shit.

Big five-oh treat.

Bella (*disgusted*)   *Mamma Mia*?

Col   Taste's in her arse, eh?

Kept non-stop nipping Dad's ear about how getting a ticket's 'top of my Before-the-Sands-of-Time-Run-Out wish list' till the poor old bugger took the hint.

Bella   Aww.

Col   Aww, nothing.

Bella   Aww, it's romantic. Your dad's made her wish come true. Mind you, 'f my time was running out, wouldn't want to sit through a shite musical with a grumpy man and hunners of women having hot flushes and all giving it (*sings*) 'you can dance'.

Swim with dolphins. At least.

Beat.

Let you come with me.

As **Col** *turns back into the room* **Bella** *is trying to conceal the broken record down sofa.*

Bella   Would you like that, Col?

She cuts her hand on record.

Aw!

Col   Huh?

Bella   You and me swimming with dolphins before your time runs out.

Col   Is running out.

After tonight.

Bella   Nah, she'll be all loved up after her romantic weekend away. Sashay back in here a brand new woman.

Enter **Stevie**.

Bella   Sure his mum will, Stevie?

Stevie   What?

Bella (*doing a mum-doing-Abba dance*)   Be totally walking on air after letting it all hang out at *Mamma Mia*?

Stevie (*camp, unflattering mime*)   Aye. Right up out her seat, giving it 'Thank you for the music . . . '

Letting it all hang out way more than you right now, Sonny Jim, that's for sure.

About as much fun as a lassie having a right good period.

Speaking of which –

He points at the blood **Bella** *is dripping.*

Stevie   Leaking there, Lugosi.

Col   What's that in your – ?

Bella   Nothing. Wet.

Stevie   Flooding, are you?

Col   Where's the blood from?

Bella   Nothing. Scratch. Cushion zip.

She is trying not to drip blood on sofa.

Rumpus off distracts **Col***, who goes to door.*

Col   Who the fuck invited that lot in?

Hey. Least take your shoes off 'fore you come.

Off, I said!

Male cheers off at girls' arrival.

Cries of 'drink'.

Stevie *is exiting with several bottles. Intensifying noise without.*

Stevie (*off*)   Here I come. Ready or not. Slippery Nipples and Slow Comfortable Screws coming up.

Drinks 'n' all if you're thirsty.

Got my lucky pants on, by the way.

Lucky for whoever gets to party in them.

Bella *seizes the moment alone to conceal the blood-smeared record in the sideboard drawer. As she is doing so, a letter catches her eye. She scans it, finding its contents distressing.* **Col***, looking drunker, moves back into room with* **Fiona** *and* **Lily***.* **Bella** *slams drawer shut on letter and broken record and accidentally pours advocaat into her Guinness. She is carrying the burden of her new knowledge now.*

Col   Skankers galore totally piling in here –

Lily   *Excusez-moi*!

Fiona   We're sizzling red-hot totty and you're lucky to have us.

Lily   Not as hot-looking as Colly-Wolly though.

Bella   Looking hot there, right enough, Knoxy. Me an' all.

Top's pure glued to my . . .

Ach, don't sweat it.

Any mongo shit out by? Bella's in da house.

Promise to keep things – (*'in order' gesture*).

So cheery up, eh? What's happening's happening.

Que sera sera, 'n 'at.

Lily   Yeah, cheery up. Quit being all 'it's my party and I'll cry if I want to'.

Fiona (*squawking tunelessly and rhythmlessly*)   ' . . . Cry if I want to, cry if I want to. If it happened to you . . . '

Lily/Fiona (*singing*)   ' . . . Cry if I want to, cry if I want to. You would cry too . . . '

Col   Leave it, eh?

Feel like fuckin' greeting.

Place is a tip out there. And I *promised* . . .

Fiona   Keep things nice for Mummy.

Bella   Fair dos. And we will. *I* will. Guide's honour.

Fiona   Scout's honour, surely, record-breaker?

Col   Telling you, I've been shafted big time.

Lily   Looking at me like that for?

Like you want to slita-my-throat.

Stevie says you having an Empty was so obvi, he knew you knew he knew it was party time tonight.

Bella   Come again?

Lily   Says you were telepathically dropping hints while we were singing back at assembly.

Col   Fuckin' mince. Hinted zilch.

Beat.

I'm unforgiven for this.

Bella   You'll be forgiven.

Lily   Just having some *mates* over? What's the deal?

'Four walls'll still be standing.' Isn't that your usual mantra when you're doing the climbing at someone else's party?

'Chillax. Life'll go on.'

Fiona   Anyway, your maw won't find out. Parents are thick as. Basically know fuck-all.

Col   But someone's in my mum's *bed*.

Lily   Sleeping?

Col   Yeah.

Pause.

Humping!

And on top of every wank-jock Stevie knows, the kitchen she spent all morning cleaning before she left's jammed with a crew of wasted scary bams I've never seen before –

Fiona   They'll be gone by Monday. Mummy still won't click.

Col   Won't notice the fag burns and honk of puke everywhere?

Fiona   'F she does, say you caught belly-rot offa something she left you in the fridge. Flip the guilt.

Bella   That what you'd do?

Fiona   Why not? A sudden attack of food poisoning's the best get out-of-jail card you can –

Lily   – flourish –

Fiona   – when you wake up chucking up. 'That chicken you gave me last night before I went clubbing was pure pink, Mammy, but you made me eat it all up.'

Lily   Top idea, Fi.

Bella   Ach.

*She passes **Col** her drink, which he necks.*

Bella   Roll with it, s'pose.

Your mates'll keep the lid on.

Lily   Er, guest list.

Fiona   No' polis.

Col   This room's only decorated last week.

Fiona   It is?

Bella   'S lovely, Col.

Fiona   You think?

Col   Can't let folk in. New covers.

Fiona   Really?

Col   Still to be stainproof-thingymabobbed.

Bella *surreptitiously tries to blot up the bloodstain she's left, but smears it instead, an action clocked by* **Fiona**.

Fiona   O.M.G.! Need to be pure careful nothing marks the new covers then.

Or gets broke.

Like any of those old records. Eh, Bella?

Bella   Do my best to keep a lid on for the rest of the night.

Lily   Think you should, missy!

Bella   No smokies in here for kick off. Keep it chillout –

Col   Keep it keep out.

Telly's split new and all, and tellies don't survive Empties.

Lily   Not looking at Bella!

Fiona   Or mentioning Calum Mackie's.

Nearly brained me. Punting his telly over that garage. Don't deny.

Bella   Ah, was broke already.

Fiona   Yeah, but I was busy in a bush when it came sailing . . .

Who was I busy with . . . ?

Col   Don't look at me.

Fiona   Nae danger! (*To* **Bella**.) Mad hag, so you were that night. Rampaging in they –

Fiona/Lily   – stretchy shorts.

Bella   Excuse me. That telly-fling challenge was the team's doing.

Crash. Team are singing something offensive off.

Enter **Stevie**. *He carries a dripping bottle of champagne, still gift-wrapped, and a dripping bottle of brown sauce.*

Col   Whassis?

Stevie   Kinda slightly hairy out there, people. Men-tal!

Col   Brilliant.

Bella   Hey, Col. Listen to me, right?

So in here's barred. Apart from the A-team.

Smoking outside.

Outside, Lily! Like outside this room –

Stevie   Whips this (*sauce*) off some drongo in a rugby shirt.

Col   What the fuck's he doin' with it in the first place?

Or the champagne?

Stevie   How the fuck d'I know?

Reclaimed this (*champagne*) offa some random bammy with no keks on who's hanging out a tree in your garden.

Place could be trashed here, man –

Col (*drinking*)   Gunna not remind me. Houses're always trashed at Empties. Should probbly end it.

Stevie   What? Just like that? Derrr!

Lily   Colly, you can't!

Exit **Stevie** *with sauce.*

Bella   Wee bit late now, no?

And things're calm enough –

Fiona (*at window*)   Calm?

Garden out there's a cross between a public toilet and a porno set!

One – two – three bare spotty white arses bobbing up and down and in and out the bushes like there's some kinda humping contest going on we've not entered in time.

Lily (*at window*)   You're right, Fifi!

Hey, and old Mr Colostomy Bag's well in there filming.

Col   Brilliant.

Lily (*at window, rolling cigarette*)   Hilarious.

Bella   Oi. What d'we say?

Bella/Col   No smoking in here.

Lily   'No smoking in here!' God's sake, Colly! Where's the harm in a few puffy-wuffs while you 'n I are having a nice –

Col   Please, not in here –

Lily   – quiet chit-chat. Isn't that what you wanted? 'Just us. All weekend.'

Beat.

Not even a ciggy-ciggy.

Fiona   Tut. Tut.

Lily   And Mama's never going to sniff out one little herbal. Come on.

Col   Not in the mood.

Lily   Put you in the mood.

Bella   You heard.

Col   Leave it. Don't be smoking that outside either.

Fiona   How not?

Col   Mr Berry.

Fiona   He's other things on his porny old mind.

Lily (*knocking window*)   Not now. Ooh, he's looking.

Helloo, Mr Humpy-back. Great cardi!

Fiona   Wanna party down, Grandad? (*Flashing.*)

Malfuction your pacemaker for you.

Take you into the bush and show you mine.

Bella   Per-lease. Have you no limits, hen?

Col   Come away, fuck's sake. See if he catches one dodgy sniff? Speed-dial it to the polis –

Fiona   Should give the wee hobbly goblin something worth cliping, then.

Girl snog?

Me and you, Lily, talking b.t.w. Not you.

Got some limits, hen.

Bella   No fear.

Fiona   But you can film him gowping on my moby so we can tag him a perv. *That*'ll keep him schtum.

She exits.

Bella   Wants watching that one. Stirrer.

Lily   I'll tell her.

Bella   Leaves a trail.

Lily   *She* leaves a trail? That's rich from Bella the telly totaller.

Bella On my best behaviour.

Enter **Stevie**.

Stevie Hubba-hubba. Ten little maids. Thirteen. Fourteen. Don't know which way's up. Pure stoat of pigtails and alcopops.

Squealing off.

'All, comin' up'.

Col All wasted? Shit.

Stevie Shit nothing. Open season for us big boys, eh?

Col Eh. Pass.

Bella Get totally sparkled at that age. Always messy.

Col Cheers for that.

Better not be traipsing through puddles of bloody puke –

Stevie (*at window*) Ooops!

Bella Sit tight, party boy.

Exit **Bella**.

Lily Well, well. So much for 'just you and – '

Stevie Ooo-ee-ooh!

Col *Was* meant to be just . . .

You said . . .

He advances.

Stevie Gwan, my son.

Col Could try and get rid –

Stevie And pigs like Bella might fly.

Col Make it just . . .

Lily *retreats.*

Lily   No thanks. Massive party crowd's much better.

But shame you didn't put the word out sooner.

Stacks won't know it's happening.

Col   Nothing should be happening.

Lily (*texting*)   Hang on. Marianne. Erin.

Col   Must you?

Lily   Oooh, and is Rachel here . . . ?

As **Lily** *opens the door to exit,* **Bella** *barges in, colliding with* **Lily**, *thoroughly splashing her and the sofa with Guinness.*

Lily   My top!

Stevie   Heifer.

Col   Not the sofa!

Col *and* **Bella** *both dive at sofa.* **Col** *to whip cushion away,* **Bella** *to stop* **Col** *seeing any pieces of the broken record.*

Lily   Ooh Bella, that's going to stain.

Bella   Well, get a cloth!

Lily   Not *my* Guinness all over the new covers.

Col   Blood on this too.

Bella   Just a splodger.

No worries. I'll sort it – quick.

Bella *conceals the broken record behind a cushion she picks up. She dives over to sideboard, shoves the record in a drawer and opens a bottle of champagne, dripping a fizzing trail en route to tipping it over both the Guinness and blood stains.*

Col   What the fuck you . . . ?

Stevie   Steady the Buffs, Bells!

Bella   Solvent.

Stevie   For red wine, you spanner.

Bella/Col   Shit.

Bella   Col, I'm so . . .

Man, what'm I like?

Swear I'll pay to get it all dry-cl –

Col   For Monday?

Enter **Lily**.

Lily   *Rachel*'s here. Off her face.

Stevie   Greasy-chops, fake-tan, horse-laugh Rachel?

Col   Cloth?

Lily   Ooops!

Bella   And salt.

She belts out. Offstage she is heard shouting for people to make way.

Enter **Fiona**.

Bella *belts back in with a towel and a tub of salt, which she pours liberally on the stains.*

Bella   No. Scary Rachel.

Flat out upside down on your stairs so she is. Skirt rid up to her oxters.

'Soooo shitfaced. Just downed a bottle of voddy on the 66.'

And I'm Scarlett Johanssen.

Stevie   Before her sex change.

Fiona (*exiting*)   You're funny, Stevie.

Bella (*mopping up, smearing the stains*)   Yon mad darty stare going on across the eyes already.

Look. Brand new.

Nearly.

Col   And once it's dried in, think you just hoover?

Stevie   Get Kim and Aggie. More like nearly new, slightly soiled to me.

Bella/Col   Aw!

Lily (*at door*)   There's Rachel bubbling.

Nihilistic banshee howling imminent.

Stevie   'Everyone hates me.'

Give it half an hour, be phoning Mummy: 'I want to come home now.'

Col   Perfect! Rachel's old dear grassed us to the cops at Stumpy Pauline's –

Bella   Only cuz we were crawling.

Lily (*to* **Col**)   You in particular, though doubt you'll remember.

Stevie   Gonged out my tree an' all that night.

Tried to drag Rachel's haggy-troll mother up to dance –

Bella   Haggy-troll mother got half Stumpy's lifted.

Be happening again, Knoxy, 'f she takes a dekko in your kitchen.

Not to freak the party, but few dodgy schemies doing *lotta* dodgy shit.

Exit **Bella**.

Stevie (*sings*)   'She'll do anyfing, for you, Col. Anyfing . . . '

Col   Shit, how d'you get schemies out your house?

Stevie   Offer them champagne?

Lily (*holding up albums*)   Play a medley of this?

Col   Serious, man.

Stevie   Pray?

Lily   Look at you, so worried.

Pause.

Weren't worrying at Stumpy's.

Stevie   Full-on schemie yourself.

Enter **Bella**.

Stevie   'Member, Col? Stumpy's?

Bella   Fried. 'Excuse me, constable, many times you wank off watching – '

Bella/Stevie/Lily   – *Babe*.

Bella   Lucky those meaty cops were more interested in yon mental tooled-up MSN gate-crashers.

Speaking of which –

Stevie   Posh-school Cedrics in the leather coats?

Lily   With the chains!

Col   Please don't tell me.

Bella   Just pointing out, front door's still gaping. I'd be out there 'cept you need a mate protecting everything in here more –

Stevie (*aside*)   Aye, like I need a perforated bowel –

Bella   – but at the same time, last thing you want's an invasion of droogs, Col.

Lily (*at door*)   Hey, speaking of Stumpy . . .

Bella   Aye: stoating. Topless. Not a pretty sight.

Stevie   Pot. Kettle. Black.

Lily (*at door*)   Oooh. She's dragging Billy Dick upstairs.

Stevie   This I gotta see.

Lily   Follow me.

Exit **Lily**.

Col   He's not going upstairs all sick, is he?

Stevie (*at door*)   Doesn't know where he's going. Gurglin'

G'luck, Billy. Nice knowing you!

Exit **Stevie**.

Col (*calling after* **Stevie**)   Gunna just check what's what, eh?

Bella   Warning you. Kitchen? Footie boneheads giving it heavy ned-mince: 'Aw right man. Sorted, 'n 'at. Any good shit?' And there's a huddle of trakkies conferring 'bout whether or not to take it the wrong way.

Enter **Stevie** *with box of cereal*.

Col   Well?

Stevie (*offering* **Col** *cereal*)   What?

Enter **Lily**.

Lily   Some sca-a-a-ry people in this house!

Col   Fuck.

Lily   Just drinking.

Stevie   And staring?

Lily   One of them emptying cereals.

Col   On the floor?

Stevie   Not this packet.

Lily   Yeah. No. Well, over someone lying on the floor.

Would've said stop, 'cept they were kind've all looking me up and down like . . . (*Intimidating glare.*)

Col (*bracing for exit*)   Perfect.

Lily   And some guy in a leather coat's sorta painting.

Col   Leather coat?

Bella   Painting!

Stevie   'S awright.

Just with ketchup.

Lily   And that brown sauce –

Col   And you let him?

Lily   It's not *my* Empty!

Col   Man!

Bella   Hey, less stressing Party Boy here.

We all blitz this place back to how it was tomorrow.

Col   Never be back to how it was.

Lily (*out on patio smoking*)   Er. F.Y.I. Packing tomorrow.

Bella   Can spare an hour.

Lily   Be plenty helpers. Make everyone who crashes –

Col   Hey, nobody's crashing.

Stevie   Wouldn't bet.

Lily   Anyway, the aftermath's tomorrow's problemo.

And tomorrow never comes.

Bella   Shite.

Stevie   Technically it doesn't.

Lily   So why worry when the night is young, and so are you . . . ?

Stevie   This clever girl talkee my language.

Lily   Just play some decent music, Col. How about it?

Dance. Get wasted.

(*To* **Col**.) You like getting wasted.

Stevie   Clever girl really talkee my language.

Lily   Should all get totally wasted.

Stevie   Sparkled.

Col   Go easy, Lily. 'S not shandy.

Lily   ''S not shandy.' Play yourself back.

Not exactly Percy Prude at other parties.

Stevie   First out of it.

Bella   Last to leave.

Stevie   'Totally lost in space, man.'

Lily   Oooh, speaking of oblivion –

See tonight, when Mum panic-phones –

Bella   This'll be about four a.m. 'Isobel? Lily's not in her bed, Isobel.'

Bella/Lily   We're sleep-overing.

Stevie (*sings*)   'Beauty and the beast.'

Lily   And still speaking of oblivion, any chance of a private prescription, Doctor Feelgood?

Col   Forget that here!

Bella   Not learned anything from having your own striker running out mega-mongoed in front of a bus thanks to your happy pills?

Stevie   He thought he was being chased by a Mars bar that night.

Bella   Not that funny.

Col/Stevie   Ah, it was quite.

Stevie   Only suffered mild concussion.

Col/Bella   And flashbacks.

Lily   Well, I don't play football. So you can free my mind.

Bella   Mess it up, more like.

Lily   Grow up, Bella.

Exit **Lily** *and* **Stevie**.

Rumpus off.

Col   Shit.

Bella   Stay put.

(*At door.*) Hey, so laughing boy's packing.

Col   'S not right having Stevie dishing shit . . .

Bella   Shit like you bought last time he was dishing.

Then dropped in my dad's car?

Who's no angel when it's not his problem, Knoxy-Knox?

Col   Wasn't dealing in your house.

Bella   'S not like your mum's installed CCTV.

Col   Stranger things've happened.

Bella   Ach, anyway, this is kinda what we do our age.

Act like numpies cuz it's in the script.

Beat.

Actually, see my mum? This caper, Col?

Have me dead and buried.

Pause.

Torture me slow first.

Col   Aw, cheers, Bella! Feel a lot better now.

Bella   Listen you: at the enda the day, hardly life and death this.

What's a few beer bottles in the washing machine?

Col   Sticky floors?

Bella   A broken record?

Col   Nah. Whoof. That's pushing it.

Bella   Yeah?

Col   Oh, God, aye.

Break one and –

Dad.

Is.

Going.

To . . .

Bella   Hey. But your dad's decent enough.

Up to plenty high jinks himself, betya.

Col   Joking.

Beat.

Boasts he was never a teenager.

Glass shatters off. Yelling etc.

Col *flinches.*

Bella   So know what, pal? Howz about just trying to –

Col   What?

Bella   – enjoy what you've got while you've got it.

Col   Huh?

Bella   Few mates. Few drinks . . .

Bella even let you dance with her if you ask nice . . .

Stuff spills, we mop up. Make a fingertip search for used
jonnies after –

Col   Aw, please, no! Don't even go there.

Window is thudded.

That so better not be Stevie's jocks playing blindfold goalie.

'Member those patio doors at that last party? Panned.

Bella (*at window*)   'S awright; just a big numpty kicking.

Pause.

Oi, away toe that up your own backside, sunshine.

Col   Kicking?

Bella   Tennis ball. Not a proper football.

See? Every Empty's different.

Some are crap.

Some are mental.

Some are scary.

This one? Feels . . .

Kinda like you could pair up with someone you mibbe don't imagine you'd –

Col *footers around with the records.*

Col   Lily's gone ages. Better check she's . . .

Bella   Hey. On guard. In here. You and me?

Col   Aw, but I'm not leaving these, case some stompin' balloon . . . Wrecking. Nicking. Sicking.

Bella   Like at my sister's? She didn't've a spare pair of knickers to her name after that flat-warming.

Underwear fed through every letterbox up the close.

Col   'S what happens. The ritual.

Same as how you wake the neighbours when you're chucked out.

Push your mongoed mates home in wheelie bins when taxis won't carry them –

Bella   Only shitey-whitey themselves carry on like –

Gagging off.

Speaking of the . . .

Col   Man!

Bella   Sit tight. I'll put a bucket on standby.

She exits.

Bella (*off*)   Oi, not the stairs.

Out 'n pish in the bushes if you gotta go.

Aw, not in the vase neither.

Increasing volume offstage.

Col   Man, do I wish I was being pushed in a wheelie bin somewhere else right now?

Out my head. Gone.

He slumps at the window, looking out, drinking. Enter **Stevie**. *Not seeing* **Col**, *he beelines to records and sifts through them.*

Stevie   Oi, gunna leave the wee lassie be, Lugosi?

Pishing canny harm the flowers.

Bella (*off*)   Big spotty arses break vases, but.

China breaking. **Col** *rushes to door.*

Col (*to someone outside room*)   Aw. Least pick the pieces up.

Beat.

Is my fuckin' house, actually.

Beat.

No you fuckin' can't come in here.

Col *fends people off in doorway before noticing* **Stevie** *and diving over to tussle with him over a Billie Holiday record.*

Col   Oi. Leave that, told you.

Stevie   Where's the fuckin' dance beats here?

Gotta be *something* 'part from this old junk.

Col   Classic that. Break it, you can 'fess it to my dad.

Stevie   Fuck that. Be an accident.

Col *returns to the door as it's kicked open.*

Col   Oi. Out.

(*To* **Stevie**.) Still need to replace what's broken.

Stevie   Nothin's getting broken.

Getting some fuckin' party sounds in here's all I'm doing.
'Right here, right now . . . '

Stevie, *dancing, stands on the record. Hastily conceals it in the drawer.*

Enter **Lily**, *unsteady and all over* **Stevie** *as she helps him choose a CD or music on one or other of their iPods that's hi-energy, trancy, throbbing.*

There is a discordant clash of sound.

Lily (*dancing*)   What d'you really make me swallow, Stevie?

Stevie   Sweetie for sweetie. Yeah, baby. 'I love the way you move.'

Lily   No, really.

Stevie   Something to get you tripping.

Lily   No!

Stevie *trips* **Lily** *into his arms.*

Stevie   Course I didn't. I'm baad-ass, not evil.

Something to turn y'on, that's all.

Make you dance like you're dancing now.

Make you wanna wrap your arms . . .

Stevie *and* **Lily** *dancing.* **Stevie** *increasingly intimate.*

Lily   Ste-*vie*! Just dance.

Stevie   Come on. Tomorrow never comes. Sez it yourself.

Seize the day.

Won't get another chance to feel me up all summer.

You'll miss me.

Lily   Sez who?

Stevie   Sez your body: 'Take me, baby. I'm yours.'

Lily   Ste-*vie*. You're bad.

Stevie   Ya love it.

Lily   You're naughty.

Stevie   Naughty, naughty.

Music drives on.

Stevie *persists.*

Lily *gradually succumbs and the pair begin kissing,* **Lily** *awkwardly aware of* **Col***'s presence in the doorway,* **Stevie** *playing to it.*

Increasing noise off, **Col** *yelling at guests from doorway.*

Lights flicker on the scene and music stutters as **Stevie** *and* **Lily** *grow more passionate.*

Exit **Lily** *and* **Stevie***, crossing* **Col** *as he dashes to the record player, a broken vase in his hand.*

A record is going on the turntable at the wrong speed.

The lights trip and the music stops abruptly.

The power cut, soundtracked by an intense, percussive backbeat, allows unidentified '**Guests**' *to invade the sitting room.*

A wild chaotic scene plays in silhouette, giving the impression that there are many people in the room.

Include improvised 'Rachel' wailing off: 'I should never have come here. Stop feeling me up. I don't like it', etc.

Also improvised outbursts from **Col***, warning people to leave the records alone, calm down etc.*

Fiona   Ey, quit jabbing at my tits, moany freak. Away, commit suicide or something. 'M busy.

Muffled Unidentified Male   She's busy.

Bella   Ey. Big man.

Slam elsewhere. New covers on that sofa.

Female Voice   Wanna phone my mum.

Col   What's wrong with the lights?

Sobby Female Voice   Where's my mobile?

Col   And gunna everyone shut the fuck up two seconds.

Fiona   You're the one making the rammy.

Bella   Oi.

'S not a trampoline.

Col   Get a torch, someone.

Groping pointlessly here.

Bella   Said not a trampoline!

Male Voice   Not that pointlessly.

Fiona (*off*)   Heh, paws off the arse an' all.

Deep, Drawly Male   Apologies, doll.

Bella   Hearing me, pal?

Fiona   Oooh, are you the biker guy!

Bella   Right, that's it.

Col   Any sign of a torch yet?

Fiona   Wanna take me riding?

Stevie   And Raleigh Chopper's straight in there!

Bella   Aye. Am talking to you, by the way?

Problem?

Stevie   Making an orgy out of a crisis.

Col   Gunna please try mind those records, people?

Bella   You heard.

Aw, that's it.

Party elsewhere.

Room's barred.

C'mon, all out.

Others improvise objections.

Lily   Oooh. This dark's sooo freaky.

Stevie   I know.

Col   Still really need a torch.

Kitchen's full of knob-ends using the gas rings for light.

Lily (*whisper*)   Gunna please just keep the mitts off my tits two seconds. Better help Col.

Stevie   How? Not your *boy*friend.

Wet farting sound.

Bella!

Beat.

Is he?

Bella   Wasn't me.

Just parked on something squashy.

Stevie   And that's news all of a sudden?

I'm your boyfriend tonight.

Bella   Explains the honk of HP sauce.

Ey. Move.

Stevie   Lovely!

Bella   How we doing, Col?

Oi, big man.

Fag.

Out.

Lily   You think you're my boyfriend do you?

Col   Still can't see a thing.

Stevie   What am I then? Friend with b-i-i-g benefits? Fill in fu –

Lily (*whisper*)   Ste-*vie*. Bad boy.

Bella   So get helping Col, people.

Ey! Where you wheeling that telly? Back here, you.

She apprehends and finally ejects various silhouettes in a scuffle.

Try coming through that door again, you'll know all about it.

No idle threat, by the way. I kick-box.

(*Off.*) How we doing, Col?

Col   Still looking.

Not seen Lily either.

Bella (*off*)   I'm under the kitchen sink now.

Stevie   Won't find her there, pie.

Bella   Now I'm checking the sideboard.

Oh! Drawer's missing.

Col   What?

Bella   Trying the other. Nothing long or hard yet –

Stevie   What you expect when it's your pudgy paws groping, Lugosi?

Lily   Ste-*vie*!

Stevie   Awch! Stomped my shin, you heifer!

Bella   Quit humping at my feet then.

Lily   Shhh.

Col   Lily?

Lily *smothers giggles.*

Bella   Yo! Candle!

Just need a match now.

Stevie   Eas-y. Bella's face and a cowpat.

Or Bella's mug and Shrek's arse –

Lily   Ste-*vie*!

Bella   Away fling shite at yerself, Stevie. News coming in: not exactly Playmate of the Month. Whatever legless wee desperado you're getting down and dirty with there, she's in for the fright of her life when the lights come on and she clocks where her hands've been.

Be wishing she'd a tube of that antiseptic swine-flu gel –

Lily   *Excusez moi*, Bella!

Bella   Help ma boab, Lily. Goin' ugly early?

Exit **Bella**.

Col *at door.*

Stevie   Hark the expert.

Bella (*off*)   Here we go!

Stevie   Take your time.

Main switch thrown on and off showing stage action through stroby flashes. During this, **Bella** *starts singing 'This little light of mine/ I saw the light'.* **Stevie** *and* **Lily** *coming up for air to join in mockingly.*

Col *drunkenly chips in as he lurches about the room.*

*During the singing any final non-cast '***Guests***' exit, policed by* **Bella***, who clatters into telly just as lights snap on properly.*

Bella   Ooops. Tripped.

No damage, but.

Stevie   Godzilla strikes again!

Col   No damage, uh?

The sitting room is trashed: sofas tipped over, one smeared in brown sauce, **Stevie** *and* **Lily** *under the other, records strewn, broken contents of sideboard drawers scattered. As* **Col** *picks through them he finds the broken records and a sheaf of letters.*

Col   Aw, pigsty, man. And dad's Sarah Vaughan!

And his Billie!

Bella   Hell's bells!

Col   Fuck!

Shit!

Lily (*on hands and knees*)   What's this? Oooh, there's loads.

Stevie   'Private and confiden – '

Bella   Neb out, that means.

Lily   Oooh, all from hosp . . . (*Reads.*) 'Oncology – '

Stevie (*in synch*)   Oink, oink.

Col   'Oncology . . . '

Hey, these are Mum's.

Stevie   Lemme guess. Extreme makeover?

Sex change? Clap clinic?

Bella   Ho. Quit. Gunna.

Lily   Ste-*vie*. Behave.

Col   Hey, what you up to on the floor anyway?

Bella   Good question for a lady.

Stevie   Yeah. Why, Lily?

Lost something?

Bella   Sensa taste for kick off.

Lily   Just resting.

Stevie   Ultrasound, this. Gutted.

Mumser's up the duff, means, dunnit?

Lily   Eeeoww!

Bella   Guys, really –

Col   Behave.

Stevie   Wee Fireman Knox still pumping away with his
hose –

Lily   Eeeoww!

Bella   Aw please, just zip it for once, willya?

Col   Mind, sicko? Check this: radiotherapy.

Fuck.

Zat not what happens when you've got . . .

Pause.

Col   Is, in't it?

Bella (*quick*)   Oh, not necessarily –

Stevie   Says Doctor Bella MD.

(*Reading.*)   Fuck, mate. You're worried about hiding the evidence of a wee *party*.

Lily   Ste-*vie*!

Col/Stevie   Fuck.

Bella *tries to exchange 'change the subject' glares with* **Stevie** *and* **Lily**.

Lily *drags* **Stevie** *down and gestures for him to keep schtum.*

Bella   Right. Listen, I'd tidy these back. Way they were, Knoxy. Help you.

Col   Way they were? (*Reading*) Hold on. This one here's for . . .

Fuck.

Bella   Says admission.

Beat.

Awright. (*Taking letter.*) Definitely put them away safe.

And sure your mum's not said anything about this?

Col   What?

Pause.

That she's going into . . .

Enda next *week* –

Stevie   Hel-lo! Another Empty!

Lily   Ste-*vie*!

Bella *takes letters from* **Col**.

The others watch while she replaces them with great care in the drawer.

Col *drinks, watching too.*

As soon as the letters are out of sight, he sweeps everything from the sideboard.

Bella/Lily/Stevie   Hey! / Ooooh! / Pal!

From this point there should be a marked recklessness to **Col**'s *behaviour.*

Col   Ho, people, wassup with y'all?

That's the power's sorted and mosta the mentalists you brought in pure totally got tae *fuck* –

Bella   Bella style. No need to thank me –

Col (*dumb voice*)   Ta, Bella.

Awright, so, while the Happy Gang's still here, gunna let's us do a fuckin' party game or something.

Stevie   Woop-de-do. Musical bumps?

Bella   Game. Sure.

She is glaring at **Stevie**.

Bella   'Specially since the vibe's kinda gone a bit – (*Blows raspberry.*)

Col   Say that again!

He blows a massive wet raspberry as he spirals about the room.

Down to the fuckin' depths.

Not zactly in keeping with any fuckin' party I should be having? Eh? Eh?

Stevie   Ea-sy, pal.

Bella   Earth to Col. OK. So we play a game.

In here. That way we can still keep your mum's good room –

Lily   Ship-shape?

Col   Shit-shape.

Pause.

Why not? (*Sings loudly.*) 'It's my party', after all.

C'mon. Everyone! Sing my party song.

Lily, **Stevie** *and* **Bella** *sing reluctantly to* **Col**'s *conducting with clashing bottles. Others lack enthusiasm and song peters out.*

Col (*very loud*)   'Cry if I want to. You would cry too if it happened to . . . '

C'mon. Kinda game, but? Waiting.

Bella   Drinking obvi.

'Less you got your pocket Scrabble handy. Nah?

Col   Twister somewhere –

Lily   Oooh . . .

Stevie   Hel-lo! S'long as it's more chicks than dicks.

Bella   Dodgy playing Twister with me. Tendency to parp out –

Collective groans.

Col (*demonstrating*)   Heh, heh. Pure choking Bella smella toxic mushroom clouds every time you hoik your leg: 'Gas! gas! quick boys . . . '

Stevie   More chicks than dicks, said.

Not chicks with dicks.

Lily   Ste-*vie*!

Col   Ch-ching! Robbed the words right out my mouth there Stevie boy. Ha, ha, ha . . .

Lily   Boys! Be nice.

Col   'Be nice.' I'm always nice.

Ho, and Bella's used to it. Eh, pal?

Lily   I know, but all the same.

Sometimes you just turn a bit –

Col   What?

Lily   You know what: O.T.T.

Col   Just ribbing. In't I, Bella? Bit a fun.

Bella   Sure. And mince from pies like you guys flies straight over my head.

Can take it.

Thick skin.

Stevie   Hide.

Col/Stevie   Boom-boom!

Col   People. People. People. What we playing? What we playing? What we playing?

Stevie   Awright, awright.

Lily   Col, careful!

Bella   Howz about Bladder Burst?

Recap: c-r-u-s-h your bladder hard as it goes against the carpet and try not to pish or burp.

Bella *necks a pint as she demonstrates.*

Col *chimp-grunts accompaniment.*

Stevie   Aw, not yon stupit home-knitted –

Lily   – so-called 'game' I can't even play cuz I don't drink pints in case you haven't noticed, Bella –

Col/Stevie/Bella   Cuz 'I'm a lady'.

Col   Same as my mummy.

He minces about pretending to straighten the room.

Stevie   And Bella wins hands down cuz her bladder's bigger than a septic tank.

Col   Industrial-scale septic tank. Slosh. Slosh. Ha, ha, ha, ha . . .

Lily *gasps.*

Bella *is necking second pint, encouraged as before by* **Col** *until* –

Bella   One–nil!

Hey, pished yourself last time you played me, Col, 'member?

Col (*squaring up*)   Did I fuck, man! Did I fuck!

Bella   Awright.

Lily   Col!

Bella   Sorry. You didn't.

But someone at Stumpy's did. While I was flat out on Stumpy's mattress.

Stevie   Probbly pished yourself. Talking of pish . . .

He exits.

Bella   Not me, no way!

Two–nil!

She is lining up pint number three.

I'm no lightweight.

Lily   Say that again.

Col (*lumbering*)   Say that again.

Bella   Awright, awright.

Pause.

But look at you all, eh?

Talking your way out of drinking. Same as last time.

Six pints down before I was begging for mercy.

Couldn't walk.

Col   Tell me about it!

Slipped a disc lumping you to the cludgie.

Lily   Don't really want to play a drinking game.

Bella   Find something better to play under that sofa then?

Col   Why you hiding anyway?

He tips sofa over.

Lily   Who's hiding?

Just chillin'

Bella   Chillin'?

Col (*singing falsetto like Travolta, only borderline screaming*)   'On a hot, su-u-u-mer night . . . '

Lily   And I was looking for you, Col.

Bella   Head first down Stevie's keks?

Enter **Stevie** *with fireman's helmet.*

Stevie (*to* **Lily**)   Wanna see the floor show up the stairs.

Col   Floor show?

Stevie   A bike taking a biker for a ride. No joking.

(*To* **Lily**.)   Your shameless BF giving it bucking bronco in her scanties and this.

Ding-dong.

Col   Yee-ha!

Beat.

Oi! Where'd she get the helmet but?

Col *takes helmet from* **Stevie**, *clonking him with it.*

Stevie   Ea-sy!

Lily   Or a biker?

Bella   Don't know any bikers.

Stevie   Just bikes.

Stevie/Col   Like Raleigh Chopper.

Lily   Fio-na!

Col (*exiting with helmet on*)   Better bloody not have taken any more of my dad's gear.

Stevie   Me-maw, me-maw. Panic stations. Where's the fire?

Bella   Leave it.

Stevie   What've *I* done?

Bella   Just leave it.

(*Quietly.*) See how he's cranking himself up?

Stevie   So what's new there?

Knoxy's inner beast is stirring, that's all.

Bella   Nah, but more of an edge to the way he's . . .

Ah, poor guy just probably just canny handle . . .

Mean, see those *letters* . . . ?

Lily (*quiet*)   I know. His mum must be totally si –

Stevie   Looks like –

Stevie *makes throat slit / hanging from a noose gestures as* **Col** *enters, helmet on squint.*

Bella   Col. Careful.

Col   How?

Bella   Stoating about, bashing that off every surface in the room including my shoulder, that's how –

Col   So? 'S not your helmet.

Why you worrying?

Lily   Your dad's helmet, isn't it, Col?

Maybe should –

Col   And 's not your house.

Can do what I like here.

'S my house. Right?

Bella   Awright.

Col   Bash what I fuckin' like.

See. Bash. Bash. Bash.

Lily   Col!

Stevie   Ey, pretty well dunted anyway, innit?

Daddy Knox play the superhero wearing it or something?

Bella   Did he, Col?

Lily   Col? Stevie's talking to you.

Stevie   Betya.

(*Film trailer voice.*) 'All Fireman Knox knew in his heart, was he gotta battle those flames, that smoke and them crashin' down beams. Forget his own safety. Just pull the darn-tootin' kids out that ragin' inferno . . . '

Bella   You and your hilarious voices, Hepburn.

Should be doing stand-up –

Stevie   Tell me about it.

Seriously. People keep saying –

Bella   – on some Freeview channel that's permanently scrambled.

Col   Desert island.

Stevie   Jealousy's a terrible thing, Lugosi. Eh, right lines too, Knoxy, eh? Eh! Knew it! I'm good.

(*Falsetto.*) 'And everyone knows that you're my hero.'

Should be on *X-Factor*.

Entering next year for sure –

Bella   What?

Stevie   What what?

My wee maw says –

Bella   Lemme guess: you'll win hands down, no contest –

Stevie   Aye, as a matter of fact.

Col/Bella   No chance.

Stevie   B-i-i-i-g chance.

Anyway, so what's the story, Jackanory?

Daddio wear this saving lives, Knoxy?

Col   Some.

Lily   Wow.

Where?

Col   If you can call dragging a wardful of incontinent veggies out some old folks' saving *lives*.

Lily   Aw, Col.

Col   Fuck, why gee it for *any*one in God's waiting room.

Their number's up –

Bella   Col, you know you don't really mean that.

Stevie   Let 'em fry. Make way for us beautiful youth.

Col   Fry!

Lily   Ste-*vie*!

Stevie   What?

Bella   Think you'll ever grow up?

Stop pissing people off?

Stevie   Hope not.

He is pulling his **Bella** *face.*

Stevie   Cuz the look on your big righteous Halloween cake of a gommy face is so fuckin' hilarious.

Anyway: proper party game time.

Col   Come on, then. Upferrit!

Enter **Fiona** *in* **Col**'*s mum's underwear.*

She looks stoned.

Stevie *and* **Col** *instinctively wolf-whistle and pant.*

Col/Stevie   Kinda game I'm talkin' about!

Fiona   Seen ma top?

Bella   Never mind your *top*, hen.

Col/Stevie (*high-fiving*)   Never *mind* your top.

Col   Oi, but where d'you get those pants?

Fiona   Not *agent provocateur*, that's for sure.

Hey, pure junky by the way, your mum.

Granny-knicker drawers hoaching with tablets.

She holds out pills.

Col   Not my mum's. Never takes any . . .

Beat.

Tablets for what?

Fiona   Christ knows.

Must be bi-i-i-g pain, cuz I'm feeling none right now.

Pure nodding out.

Col   Alright!

He takes some pills from **Fiona***, opens and closes helmet visor to speak/take pill in the following.*

Bella   What you doing?

Lily   Col!

Stevie (*to* **Fiona**)   Astronaut.

Bella   Space cadet. Pair of you.

What happens if those pills you've necked're to do with –

Col   What? Mum's fuckin' secret everyone knows about?

Fiona   Er. Not me, thanks a bundle.

Bella   Just necked pills his mum needs.

Can't believe you. Sick.

Fiona   I'm sick?

What about Host-with-the-Most here?

Should know better if it's his own maw on this good shit.

Bawl *him* out.

Col   Try it.

Fiona   Just looking for my top!

Was on your bed. But canny get in your room.

Col   Come you can't get in my room?

He drops visor.

See about that!

Fiona   Sez who? Oh, hello in there. Still hiding away.

Hey, no wonder. Seen your kitchen?

In-sane.

Pure giant edible Art Attack all up the walls.

I licked it.

Bella   Good for you!

Fiona   No, not really. Mustard.

Hey, this Empty's pure mental, by the way.

She picks up photo of **Col** *with his mum.*

Fiona   Think you'll be getting many more smiles like that offa her?

She's pure gunna die off!

Bella/Stevie/Lily *blanch.*

Col   You said it.

Bella   Awright. Enough already.

Fiona   How?

Just saying his mum's gunna die off. She is too –

Col   Is too.

Lily   Col!

Beat.

Bella   Hey, weren't we playing some game here, Hepburn?

Lily   All set.

Stevie   And you don't actually need clothes for it, Fido.

Simple rules so even big Bella can join in –

Bella   Gut-ted!

Col   Ey, why can't you get in my room?

Stevie   – called 'Who Would You Do'?

Fiona   Door's wedged, innit.

Col   Wedged?

Fiona   'Who Would You Do'?

Col   Fuckin' unwedge it, so I will.

Bella   Never heard of it.

Stevie (*dumb voice*)   That's cuz I just invented it up out my head.

Col   Duhh, Bella.

Fiona   Sounds pure cack.

Bella   Hepburn's the expert at cooking up mince.

Stevie   Stabbing, Smella. Get me a paramedic.

Col   Away to fuckin' check upstairs see who's in my fuckin' bed then gunna fuckin' brain –

Bella   You're awright, I'll go.

Col *shoves* **Bella** *back on to sofa.*

Col   *I'll* go!

He exits.

(*Off.*)   Anyone in my room, they're getting it!

Stevie   Starting to spoil my night, that wound.

Col (*off*)   Think I can't see you under the covers?

Lily   Ste-*vie*! Hey, but those letters.

Oncology means cancer.

Col (*off*)   *Is* up to me who's in here, actually.

Loud yelling, off, between **Col** *and other voices.*

Fiona   Letters?

Col (*off*)   No, I'm not gunna skip back downstairs to fuckin' sing hymns with the gay-loser-sadsacks.

Fiona   Er, and I'm not even one of the stupid gay choir sadsacks anyway, if you don't mind.

Col (*off*)   But *you're* all fuckin' out.

Pause.

So what if they're yer good jeans.

Glass shatters.

Shoes and trousers fall past window.

Bella   Bloody hell. See that?

Lily   Found all these letters.

'Bout his mum. Treatment and stuff.

Fiona   So?

Lily   There's about twenty, Fi.

Bella   She's going in for an operation.

Pause.

Shit, he's not taking it too well so far.

Stevie   As I says: the Beast awakes.

Fiona   Who?

Before *Spain*?

Whassup?

Lily   Shhh. His *mum*, not me.

Fiona   So? My mum's always getting treatment and operations.

Bella   Lemme guess: tits, eyes, tummy.

Fiona   Aye. Lipo. Arse-lift. Proper operations, but. Out for the count an' at.

Blood 'n stitches 'n shuffling about with no make-up on and one of those drips hanging down for yer piss.

Bella   *Ren*ovations not operations. Hardly *this*.

Lily   Does it actually say?

Bella   Gastro-intestinal surgery.

Fiona   Tummy tuck, then! Big wowsies.

Bella   She's not getting a tummy tuck in a cancer hospital.

Stevie   He's never said nothing.

Bella   Derr! Cuz he didn't know nothing.

You saw him with those (*letters*).

Probbly hasn't even begun to –

Lily   – compute.

Stevie   Hey.

Leaving it like that, then.

Tonight.

No point in discussing –

Bella   Oh, don't know about that. He's practically off the Richter Scale already.

Listen.

Col *bawling off* – '*Out*' *etc.*

Bella   Should mibbe sit him down. Find out how he's fee—

Stevie   Bella? Forget how he's feeling.

Have to pretend we never read a single wo—

Bella   Isn't right, but.

Doesn't feel right.

We shouldn't be here.

Fiona   How? He's got an Empty.

Why wouldn't we be here?

Bella   His mum!

She's pure sick.

Fiona   Not here, but. We are.

Young. Free. Single.

Bella   But really sick mibbe.

And to think she's sitting through *Mamma Mia*? Je-sus!

Fiona   Still not here.

Nothin' *we* can do for her anyway, is there?

Lily   Oooh.

Stevie   Fair point.

Life goes on, eh?

Lily/Bella   S'pose.

Stevie   No supposing about it. It does.

Beat.

So: 'Who Would You Do'?

Bella   Give a doing to? That's your game?

For real?

Wouldn't lamp anyone.

Beat.

'Cept maybe you, Stevie.

Aye.

Do you.

Fiona/Stevie   Oooo eeee oooh.

Lily   Bell-a!

Fiona   Lucky Stevie!

Bella   Shit.

Imagine poor Col not knowing about . . .

Beat.

No wonder he's going off his nut up there.

She exits.

Enter **Col** *dishevelled, and re-enter* **Bella** *with bag of spilling frozen peas and oven chips.*

Bella   Mammy, Daddy. That kitchen's gunna need a deeeep clean.

Col (*flinging the peas up in the air*)   Total carnage! Pwach!

Lily   Col!

Bella   Chill the chilli. Not any more.

Radio cooking in this (*saucepan*).

These (*chips*) were going round in the tumble dryer.

Col   And a window pasted upstairs.

Lily   Heard the glass going.

Col   'S awright. Only me!

Tosspots wouldn't fuck off out my bed till I chucked their shoes.

Bella   That was you?

Col   My house.

Stevie   Wild, pal.

Col (*singing in* **Stevie**'s *face*)   'Wayld thing, do roo dooo, you make ma heart sing . . . '

Stevie   Awright, down boy!

Fiona   What she's just said's wilder: 'do' Stevie.

Col   Whoa! Whoa! Whoa!

Bella   Aye, for inventing your idiot game.

Pause.

Mean who stoats around planning who they fantasise chibbing?

Fiona   News coming in, Bella. Don't actually think *do* in this –

Lily   – context –

Fiona   – means –

Bella   Duh?

Do means 'do'. Black and blue.

Fiona   Duh!

Talking 'doing' doing, but.

Stevie   Hot lurve, baby.

Lucky pants lurve.

Col *leaps on* **Stevie**.

Col   Allow me to demonstrate.

Bella   Uh?

Beat.

Ugh! That's totally . . .

Hold the bus – and you thought I meant . . .

Bella *points from herself to* **Stevie**.

Ugh! Gah!

Stevie   Don't knock the hepcat till you've tried it.

Not that you'll be getting any opportunities, Lugosi.

Anyway: game on.

Gotta tell the truth.

Fiona   Or what? Jeezo!

Col   Get a right 'doing' offa Bella.

Fiona   Kinda doing?

Stevie   Fist? Fanny? Which is worse?

Anyhoo. Come up with three names . . .

Col   Tom. Dick. Harry.

Stevie   Always had my suspicions about you, sweetie.

Col (*squaring up*)   Zat right? Suspect away.

Stevie   Joke!

Fiona   Ooooh. AC/DC.

Stevie   Oi, and not finished the rules. So one of your three's fantasy.

Col   Mean like Wolverine?

Stevie   Whatever rocks your cock, sadboy.

Col   Whassup with Wolverine? I *love* him.

Stevie   Thinking more fantasy like human you'll not likely meet.

Say, for example a nice fella with more personality than looks for you, Bella.

Shrek, mibbe.

Fiona, **Lily** *and especially* **Col** *highly amused.*

Bella   Natural born stand-up, telling you, Hepburn.

And Shrek's not human anyway.

Stevie   OK. Living fantasy superstar: Madonna, say.

Col/Bella/Fiona/Lily   Ma-*donna*?

Fiona   Pure pushing sixty.

Bella   And does she even count as human?

Col   Be like poking yer bony granny.

Fiona   And you know that how exactly?

Lily   So can your fantasy shag be dead?

Bella   You for real?

Stevie   Give me strength. Madonna's only an example, OK?

So say she's one outta your three –

Col/Bella/Fiona/Lily   Er. / Naw! / Not one of mine! / Forget it.

Stevie   Just *say*.

Other two 'do's have to be from this room.

Male. Female.

Col   Why the fuck?

Stevie   The *game*.

Col   And if you don't wanna play the game?

Stevie   *Die*, OK?

Beat.

See? Fun.

Col (*throws full can at* **Stevie**)   Fuck this for fun –

Stevie   Aw!

Bella   Calm it, Col.

Fiona   Nah. Bring it on.

Stevie   OK? Going alphabetical.

Means you're first. B for Lugosi.

Bella   I'm always first.

Stevie   Live with it.

Same as you live with how yer coupon came out God's pizza oven.

Lily   Ste-*vie*!

Col   *Stev-ie*!

Stevie   'Mon, Bella.

Obvi I'm your 'Who Would You Do' bloke –

Bella   Huh?

Stevie   Fantasy next. Me an' all, s'pose.

Bella   Living superstar?

Stevie   Watch this space.

Not that I'll be in it long. Onward and upward and all that –

Bella   – like a deflating jonnybag, aye.

Stevie   But pretend someone else if you must, Lugosi.

Bella   Arnie Swarz.

This elicits multiple impressions of Arnie, **Col** *taking the mime too far.*

Fiona   Bigger sadcase than I thought, hen.

Col   Older than Madonna –

Stevie   – and not as ripped. Seen the arms on her this weather?

Bella   Hold the bus. Picking Arnie as 'I'll be back' –

Lily   Oooh, Bel-la!

Fiona   Kinky. Robot sex.

Bella   Pul-eeze. I'd've Arnie hunt you down, Hepburn.

Do you like *I* mean 'do' – i.e. knock twelve shades of shite out you for coming up with this dipstick game.

Col (*high-fiving* **Bella**)   Love the thinking, Bella.

Twelve shades a shite! Ha ha ha . . .

Bella   Thought you might.

Col   Let's get tore in!

Col *launches himself on* **Stevie** *and pummels at him till* **Stevie** *pushes him off.*

Stevie   Awright, pal.

Lily   Ah, who'd you really do, missy?

Stevie   All on tenterhooks –

Bella (*evasive*)   You already picked.

And what exactly are tenterhooks anyway?

Stevie   Jo-king!

Pause.

OK, you're not into cock-a-doodle-dandy.

So, who'd be your chick pick?

Fiona   Don't look at me, hen.

Stevie   Not fussed, eh?

S'long as it's one or other. Aw, or both at once –

Col/Stevie (*exchanging a more elaborate shake*)   Alright!

Bella   Puh-lease! Rather you killed me.

Stevie   Cop-out Bella.

Awright, Party Animal, you're up.

Col (*growls*)   OK. Fantasy do's lovely, lovely Cheryl Cole.

Lily   Dimples like me.

Zat why you picked her, Col?

Bella   Get over yourself.

Fiona   Older woman!

Col   Fitter than *you*. Way, way, way . . .

Less skanky 'n all, Little Miss Chlamydia.

Fiona   Fuck you!

Col   Now way never.

Stevie   Ey, and nothing wrong with an older woman anyway.

Milfy, milfy!

Bella   Like you'd know.

Stevie   Ze lips are sealed.

Lily/Bella/Col   What? / Huh? / Duh?

Stevie   Saying zilch.

Beat.

'Cept there's a certain mumser.

Bella   Deffo not mine.

Col   Or mine.

The invalid.

Lily Col!

Stevie Nah, deffo not –

Fiona – from that photo.

Lily *Fi!*

Bella Aw, could you people limber any lower if you tried?

Stevie Anyhoo, this mumser's borderline do-able.

When it's late and your lucky pants've let you down –

Bella Really need to hear this?

Stevie One minute she's chinkling the ice in her voddy.

Next –

He reenacts the following with **Bella**.

Stevie – she's sliding the glass from my cheek to my jewels.

'Remember when you were yay high. Such a big boy now – '

Col/Bella Puh-lease!

Stevie ''Mon we'll've a catch up in the conservatory – '

And he scores!

Bella Fantasy island, man.

Lily Not my mum, then.

Only got a deck.

Col (*shoving* **Stevie**) Making this up anyway. Bullshit.

Stevie Oi! Am I fuck!

Wild she was: 'I'm reborn!'

Bella I'm regurgitating!

Stevie Always makes it wild if someone's grateful.

Bella Or mentally ill.

Lily   Your mum's been at your parties, Fi.

She drinks voddy and gets kinda flirty and desperate –

Fiona   What you just say?

Bella   And likes them young –

Fiona   Dissing my maw?

Col   Girrrrl fight!

Fight! Fight! Fight!

Now here's a game I do like! Bagsy ref.

Stevie   Behave.

Bella   Just stating the facts.

Fiona   You don't know any facts.

Bella   I can read between the lines –

Col   On her mum's face! (*Mimes drum roll.*)

Fiona   You dissing my mum too now?

Pause.

Least she's not rotting away fae the inside out –

This remarks stops **Bella**, **Stevie** *and* **Lily** *in their tracks.*

Stevie   Now that was low.

Fiona   Sor-ree.

Bella   Best you can do?

Fiona   Sorry, Col.

Col   For what?

Truth.

Is rotting from the inside, in't she?

Bella (*loudly, over* **Col**)   Right, people, how's about a round of Scrabble now? Or a sing-song?

Lily (*distracting* **Col** *too*)   But still Col's turn.

Col   And she never fuckin' bothered to tell me.

Cheers, Mummy! Love you.

Stevie   Quick. Chick?

Col   Aw, and she knows fuckin' fine who she is.

Fiona   Cheryl.

Lily   Moi?

Stevie   Hardly *Bella*.

Col *howls like a wolf.*

Bella   Cheers!

Fiona   Next: boy action.

Col   I'm out.

You're up, Fiona. Lassie?

Lily   Brace yourself, Bella.

Fiona   Get real. My girl's me.

Bella/Lily   Uh?

Fiona   See what makes me tick.

Stevie   *Like* your thinking.

Col   Fuckin' weird.

Gettin' a wee picture. You gettin' a wee picture, Stevie?

Stevie   Kinda. Freaky. In a kinky way.

Col   So if that's your, like, 'straight' pick, what about your fantasy?

Zit yourself in drag?

Bondage gear?

Gimp mask?

Stevie Bella mask.

Bella Ha. Ha.

Fiona Just someone minted and without plooks.

Or moobs.

Pure ginging that –

Bella – from a lassie who's been riding bareback with some leathery old *Easy Rider* dude off the street –

Col – and wants to pump herself?

Bella Can I just say, losing the will to live here, people.

Col Ditto. Ditto. Ditto. Ditto. Ditto. Dyin'. Dyin'. Dyin'. Dyin'. Dyin' . . .

Stevie Ey. Pal –

Fiona Wait, Lily's go.

Bella Fantasy?

Lily Ooooh. Head's too swimmy to think.

Stevie That's hepcat lovin' for ya.

Col What?

Bella Time up, Tinkerbell.

Stevie Hold the bendybus.

Never said *my* fantasy –

Col/Bella Madonna!

Stevie Naw. That was an example.

Pause.

Saying that, see if she was –

Bella What? Giving you the glad-eye?

(*As Madonna, singing and dancing.*) 'You look like a virgin.

Touch you for the very first time . . . '

Col, *as Madonna, joins in, knocking drinks over as he dances.*

Col   'For the very first time . . . '

Bella   'With my ru-u-ber gloves on. In the da-ark, with a bag on your head . . . '

Stevie   Experienced. Flexible.

Wouldn't say no, but wouldn't *pick* Madonna specifically –

Bella   Aw, better text her.

Col   Better, Bella.

Bella   'Dingied, hen.'

Col   'You'll get over him in time. He's got rancid halitosis anyway.'

Stevie   Have I fuck!

Col *throws himself back violently from* **Stevie** *as if in self-defence from* **Stevie**'s *breath. Scatters bottles, squishes peas etc.*

Bella   Keep the lid on, Col.

Stevie   Do not have halitosis.

Col   Ya think?

Fiona   Does anything actually *happen* in this game?

Thought we'd all be stripping at least.

Stevie   Could be arranged!

Bella   Away raffle yourself.

Col (*drinking*)   And wind this up.

Bella   Might be an idea, eh?

Lily   Awww.

Col   Naw.

Just the *game*.

Fucksake.

Do something more hardcore.

Fiona   Now you're talking, party boy!

Col   Drink till we can't see.

Or think.

Or move.

I know: tank all my mum's fuckin' cancer pills.

See how she likes that –

Bella   No, no pal.

Lily   Col.

Bella   Not really a good –

Fiona   Great idea. Shots shakedown.

Stevie   Hey, anyway, I'm still picking here.

Lily   Me too.

Hard, this.

Bella   Not if we pick for you.

Stevie's female do: Lily.

Fiona (*pointing at* **Stevie**)   Her male: *him*.

Col   Haaaa. Naaaaaa.

You think?

Stevie   Ohhhhh –

Beat.

Problemo there.

With the rule.

Col   Thought your only rule was tell the fuckin' truth?

Stevie   Impressive recall there considering you're out your tree.

Pause.

But not that rule.

Another I forgot. Ooops.

Col Tut. Tut.

Stevie Indeed.

Pause.

Cuz it disqualifies me 'n Dimples.

Fiona OK, so you're brother and sister –

Bella Like that'd put Stevie off. Pump his pet goldfish –

Col – up the jaxi without a condom –

Lily Col!

Bella – if it eyed him with any interest.

Stevie Actually, my rule's you don't pick a do you've done for real.

Pause.

Col What?

Lily *Ste-vie!*

*Exit **Lily**, upset.*

Stevie *sits on sofa, drinking and despondent, until **Fiona** sidles up. She gradually gets **Stevie***'s *attention by putting album covers up to her face.*

Stevie *and **Fiona** exit entwined.*

Bella *and **Col** sit on the other sofa, drinking.*

Bella *tries to draw **Col***'s *attention but he is unresponsive, locked down.*

She exits.

Col State of this place.

Look what they've done.

Laughing, borderline hysterical, **Col** *holds up bits of broken record trying to fit them together.*

Cowp.

Mum!

Shite.

I'm *so* dead. (*Laughs.*)

Or should that be *you* are so dead. Sucker!

Beat.

Fuck.

He puts helmet on.

Increasing noise upstairs.

Enter **Lily**.

Lily   Oooh.

Pause.

Just you?

Col (*removing helmet*)   Just me.

Looking for Stevie, were you?

Lily   Meaning, Col?

Col   Nothing.

Lily   Thought you'd be upstairs.

Col   How?

Lily   Leading the wet play.

Tanked up little party monster.

Col   Who me?

Lily   Who else?

Crazy little thing called Col.

Insane.

Col (*stilted*)   What you mean, 'insane'?

Just sitting.

Quiet.

Talking.

You and me.

Like I thought tonight was gunna . . .

Back when I said to you come round and –

Lily   *Col.*

Pause.

Mean really in-*sane*.

Up in your bathroom?

Mega splashing 'n flushing 'n plopping-

Col   *Is* the bog. Plopping happens –

Lily   Talking stuff being dropped from a height plopping.

Assumed you'd be bang smack in the thick of it. Cra-zee!

Col   Fuckin' crazy right enough.

Left to fuckin' deal with –

Beat.

Lily   No!

Oooh, I mean crazy we'll always remember how summer started when we were sixteen with Col's Empty.

Sooo crazy . . .

Col   Fuckin' insane.

I'll remember alright.

Lily   And even more totally crazy to think how me 'n Fiona'll be hundreds and hundreds of miles away on a beach in two days. Reminiscing about this wild night –

Col   – of shite I'm gunna be putting right for the rest of my life.

Lily   Oooh.

Just another little mad *soirée*.

Hey, not even *that* much worse than loads of others we've been to.

Col   You think?

Lily   I *know*.

Pause.

World's hardly coming to an end, is it?

Col   Your world mibbe.

Pause.

Mean, what about me finding all those –

Beat.

Lily   Oooh, yeah. Listen.

Beat.

Rubbish. Tough. Crap.

Sooo sorry, Col.

Col   Bit late in the day for that now!

Shit's happened.

Lily   Oh, can't say for definite yet?

Awkward pause.

Col, listen. Actually, just heading –

Col   But said you'd stay.

Lily   Kinda changed my mind.

Col   But you wanted this!

Least sit five minutes. We've hardly . . .

Lily   What?

Col   C'mon.

Thought it was just going to be –

Lily   Dunno why, Col. Honestly.

Col   Wouldn't that be . . . ?

Lily   What?

Telling pause in which **Col** *realises where he stands with* **Lily**.

Col   Aw. Lily. Stay.

Beat.

My mum's sick.

Lily   Hope it's OK with her.

Col   So stay, please.

Lily   Sure it will be?

Col   Please.

You know you really want to –

Lily (*resisting embrace*)   Do I?

She exits.

Col *in centre of room. Lost. Drinking.*

Col   How can it be OK?

How can anything be ok?

He flumps on sofa, finding brown sauce bottle, then more bits of broken record. Pounding music off highlights **Col***'s confusion and isolation as he opens the drawer to throw in broken pieces of record and lifts out the original hospital letter. Reads it, then tears it into shreds and repeats this process with all the others one by one, meanwhile drinking steadily from a can* **Bella** *left. When he is finished with the letters he takes the photograph of himself with his mum, smashes the frame, then spits drink over the photo before ripping it up.*

Col   Fuckin' hiding all this from me.

Coulda said *something*.

What am I supposed to do now?

What am I supposed to do?

He goes on the rampage.

Stevie (*off*)   Ho. Col. Anyone.

Gunna jazz it up here, gie's a hand.

Bath taps're jammed on.

Fiona (*off*)   Water's pure cascading!

Col   Flood! Whooo!

Stevie (*off*)   Need to turn it off.

Totally sluicing out everywhere.

Col   Deluge! Waaay!

Fair take your mind off your hospital appointments, that.

Fiona (*off and overlapping*)   See my shoes?

Feet're completely squelching in −eeeeow − lavvy's overflowing
now and some tube's whiteyed and not flushed!

Lights buzz, flicker, spark.

Fiona (*screeches, off*)   Pure mega-shock offa that switch now.

Near peed myself.

Col   Enda the world, Ma!

Stevie (*off*)   Never mind *your* plumbing.

Bath keeps overflowing there'll be a ceiling down.

Oi, Col. Where's yer stopcock thingy?

Col   How'd I know that?

I'm the last to know *anything* round here.

Stevie (*off*)   Col? Pal?

Doing anything about this?

Col   What the fuck am *I* supposed to do?

He makes to exit but instead sinks to the floor, puts on helmet and piles cushions round himself, forming a nest so he can't be seen.

Enter **Bella**, *tipsy.*

Lights are flickering, so she lights a candle.

Bella   Really wanna dance.

Know no one wants to dance with me, but wanna dance.

Wanna dance so much.

She chooses a record, a slow classic like Ella Fitzgerald's 'The Way You Look Tonight', and as the lights flicker down to a single beam she dances with surprising grace and sensuality, singing along to the record.

Stevie (*off*)   Gunna fuck off out and let us at the taps, people?

Fiona (*off*)   Eoiw. Like walking downstairs on sponge.

Col *sees* **Bella** *dancing.*

Col   Lily?

Bella   Not Lily.

Bella *draws* **Col** *into her spotlight.*

Col   No. C'mon.

Can't handle all this, Bella. Everything's . . .

Bella (*removing helmet*)   Shhh . . . I know.

Your mum. Too much.

But I'm here. Dance with me.

Col *and* **Bella** *dance. Clumsy at first, the dance has its 'moment' before the pair of them lose balance.* **Col** *backs* **Bella** *into the telly, which falls and breaks. Then* **Bella** *lands on top of* **Col**.

The record finishes and bumps and crackles round the turntable.

Col (*laughing bleakly*)   Not the plasma!

Bella   Sorry, sorry. Got the whirlies.

Col (*still laughing*)   Choking me, Bella.

Bella   Sorry, Col.

Sorry I broke the telly –

Col *laughs.*

Bella   And the records.

Pay everything back outta my wages.

Col (*laughs*)   That was you? You're killing me.

Bella   Swear to God. I'm sorry.

And sorry I'm not Lily.

She smothers **Col** *with kisses.*

Col *resists at first, then surrenders with a groan.*

Enter **Stevie**, *with ghetto-blaster or iPod, and* **Fiona**, *who is wearing fireman's jacket and boots.* **Stevie**, *topless, is in fireman's trousers with braces. He rifles in the sideboard and produces champagne. He turns up dance music, spraying champagne while he and* **Fiona** *dance.*

Stevie (*shouting*)   Whooo! Here's to Col's numpty maw and paw for leaving him home alone and expecting everything to stay the way it was.

Suckas!

He is tickling and licking champagne off **Fiona** *till she trips over* **Col** *and* **Bella** *under the sofa.*

Col *is already surfacing.*

Fiona   O.M.G. Stevie! How. Wellied. Am. I?

Stevie   Fuck, Col.

That's bestiality.

Col Oi. Who the fuck said you could wear my numpty dad's uniform? He'll kill you.

He pings the braces of **Stevie**'s *trousers.*

Stevie Aw, really hurt!

Fiona (*sympathy*) Listen, seeing it's your party, and your mum's like . . . y'know.

'D've been a Friend with Benefits. Save you going –

Doorbell.

Col So get the gear off.

He tussles braces off **Stevie** *while* **Fiona** *teases him to remove Dad's jacket.*

Bella *obliges, ripping a button.*

She exits.

Persistent doorbell.

Fiona Aw, now look what you've done.

Stevie (*mocking*) Yes, Fiona. put everything back zactly as you found it . . . '

Col (*pinging* **Stevie**'s *braces again*) Do it, eh?

During this exchange, the music remains loud and there's shouting off, bottles breaking, lights flickering, etc.

Enter **Bella**.

Bella Cops, Col.

Col Hurray! Cops 'n firemen. Mee-maw, mee-maw, mee-maw.

Beat.

Straight up?

Bella Looking for the person in charge.

Col *laughs weakly.*

Stevie No' find him in here!

Fiona   Can smooth-talk the polis for you, nae bother a
tother . . .

Bella   I've done it.

Fiona   Smooth-talked?

Surprised you didn't get yourself arrested for fashion crime in
that get-up.

Bella   Says the lassie in the Poundstretcher pants.

Fiona   Slagging off your fuck-buddy's sick maw there,
Pumba!

Col   Gunna please shut the fuck up.

What'm I gunna say?

Bella (*to* **Col**)   Sorted.

(*To* **Stevie**.) But music's down. Swinging back in ten to check −

Stevie   'Music's down.' Tell me what to do, awright?

He turns the music up. **Bella** *lunges.*

Bella   You deef?

Fiona   Lay off. Not tell you twice, lady.

Stevie   Lady!

Pause.

Laddy.

Bella *and* **Stevie** *tussle over music.*

Bella   Wanna see yourself, Hepburn.

Stoked like a poisoned clown now the shit's hit and your mate's
getting it big time.

With friends like you . . .

Fiona   Warned you, laddy . . .

She joins the tussle.

Bella   Hear what I said?

Cops're coming back.

Col, just so you know, been loadsa complaints.

Stevie (*shaking* **Col***'s hand*)   Sign of a mint party.

Col   I thank you.

Bella   So gunna mibbe seriously peel yourself off the ceiling now? Mosta your neighbours are out in the street –

Col/Stevie   Not asking them in?

Bella   Raging. Seriously.

Col/Stevie   Seriously.

Bella   Oh, and there's water coming down your stairs.

Col   Man! Seriously.

Bella *exiting.*

Bella   'S awright. Just gunna lay some sheets on top.

Col   Offa my bed?

Fiona   That's kinda occupied.

Stevie   Been kinda occupied all night.

Col   With.

Stevie   Lithen.

Just get you a wee litht.

Want thurnames firtht?

Stevie*'s behaviour defuses the tension.* **Fiona** *is particularly amused.*

Col   Sheets off whose bed, then?

Please not Mum and Dad's?

Doorbell. Banging off.

Enter **Bella**.

Lights flickering.

Bella   If he doesn't break this up, the cops will.

They'll be back.

Fiona (*Arnie voice / actions*)   'They'll be back.'

Col   What am I going to say?

Fiona   Know what I'd do?

Just tell them your mum's totally sick, right? Like on-the-way-out sick. And you've asked all your mates round to like block out all the worry 'n stuff pure fizzing round like in your –

Bella   D'you actually know how to zip that trap or will I show you?

Fiona   Just trying to help.

Beat.

Col   Know what? Wanna help –

Bella   – just go.

Stevie   Get tae –

He turns music up.

Bella *tries to stop him.*

Bella   No one else catching that burny smell?

Sirens.

Flashing lights of police car through window.

Water starts trickling through the ceiling.

Stevie   'I'm singing in the rain . . . '

Whoof. Know what, pal?

Prob'ly just as well your mum's in hospi next week.

My wee maw'd've a stroke coming home to this.

Bella   Electric burny smell?

Col   Aw –

He kicks out and knocks over a lit candle.

I promised . . .

Before I knew anything about her being . . .

Fiona   What?

Having her cancer 'n 'at?

Bella   Aw! You not just hear me warning you 'bout clamping that moosh?

Fiona   What did I say?

Col   I promised she'd come back and everything'd be –

Stevie   Gut-ted.

Col   I *said* no Empty.

Stevie   Don't come it. *You* wanted one too.

Col   Not in *my* house.

Kept saying, but you just went ahead.

Stevie   Lily said go for it, that's how.

Col   Lily?

Stevie   Told me you told her, 'My mum and dad've fucked off. Come play at mine. Be crazy.'

Col   Didn't mean this kinda crazy. You *know* that –

Stevie   How?

Col   But you came, anyway.

You all came. My mates.

Beat.

And now you'll all go.

Fiona   You've wanted us to go all night.

Want us to stay now? Make your mind up.

Stevie *shows others film on his mobile.*

Stevie   Want us out, suits me, cuz Slammo's sister's pal's party's melting.

Check it. Fancy?

Col   *Me?*

Stevie   Well I'm offski.

Laters.

Exit **Stevie** *swiping a bottle. Exit* **Fiona**.

Fiona (*off*)   Wait up, Stevie!

I'm with you.

Bella (*tidying ineffectually*)   Listen, you.

See tomorrow? New day.

Everything's gunna be back the way it was.

Promise –

She exits with an armful of dripping bottles.

(*Off.*) And I'm not going anywhere.

Sound of bottles dropping, off.

What'm I like?

She re-enters with black bin bag which she starts to fill.

All be sorted.

With a sparkie.

And a plumber.

Pause.

Mibbe . . . no, definitely, a glazier.

Painter.

Exit **Bella**.

Col (*addresses audience*)   You think so too?

Things can be the way they were?

Bella (*off*)   And swear to God I'll replace every broken record.

No worries.

Col   No worries.

Bella   You'll be hunky-dory for your mum coming home, Col.

Col   Hunky-dory.

Bella (*off*)   See a year from now?

Tonight'll be totally forgotten.

Promise.

Col   You think?

A fire breaks out at the sideboard.

Glass shatters off.

Music stops.

Silence apart from water running, power buzzing, cushion smouldering.

Blackout.

Methuen Drama Student Editions

Jean Anouilh *Antigone* • John Arden *Serjeant Musgrave's Dance*
Alan Ayckbourn *Confusions* • Aphra Behn *The Rover* • Edward Bond
Lear • *Saved* • Bertolt Brecht *The Caucasian Chalk Circle* • *Fear and
Misery in the Third Reich* • *The Good Person of Szechwan* • *Life of Galileo* •
Mother Courage and her Children • *The Resistible Rise of Arturo Ui* • *The
Threepenny Opera* • Anton Chekhov *The Cherry Orchard* • *The Seagull* •
Three Sisters • *Uncle Vanya* • Caryl Churchill *Serious Money* • *Top Girls*
• Shelagh Delaney *A Taste of Honey* • Euripides *Elektra* • *Medea*•
Dario Fo *Accidental Death of an Anarchist* • Michael Frayn *Copenhagen*
• John Galsworthy *Strife* • Nikolai Gogol *The Government Inspector* •
Robert Holman *Across Oka* • Henrik Ibsen *A Doll's House* • *Ghosts*•
Hedda Gabler • Charlotte Keatley *My Mother Said I Never Should* •
Bernard Kops *Dreams of Anne Frank* • Federico García Lorca *Blood
Wedding* • *Doña Rosita the Spinster* (bilingual edition) •*The House of
Bernarda Alba* • (bilingual edition) • *Yerma* (bilingual edition) • David
Mamet *Glengarry Glen Ross* • *Oleanna* • Patrick Marber *Closer* • John
Marston *Malcontent* • Martin McDonagh *The Lieutenant of Inishmore* •
Joe Orton *Loot* • Luigi Pirandello *Six Characters in Search of an Author*
• Mark Ravenhill *Shopping and F***ing* • Willy Russell *Blood Brothers*
• *Educating Rita* • Sophocles *Antigone* • *Oedipus the King* • Wole
Soyinka *Death and the King's Horseman* • Shelagh Stephenson *The
Memory of Water* • August Strindberg *Miss Julie* • J. M. Synge *The
Playboy of the Western World* • Theatre Workshop *Oh What a Lovely
War* Timberlake Wertenbaker *Our Country's Good* • Arnold Wesker
The Merchant • Oscar Wilde *The Importance of Being Earnest* •
Tennessee Williams *A Streetcar Named Desire* • *The Glass Menagerie*